Index on Censorship

Free Word Centre, 60 Farringdon Road, London, EC1R 3GA

Chief Executive John Kampfner **Editor** Jo Glanville **Associate Editor** Rohan Jayasekera **Assistant Editor** Natasha Schmidt **News Editor** Padraig Reidy **Online Editor** Emily Butselaar **Head of Arts & Events** Julia Farrington **Finance Manager** David Sewell **Fundraising Administrator** Klara Chlupata **Public Affairs Manager** Michael Harris **Sub-editor** Caroline Palmer **Interns and Editorial Assistants** Rose Gamble, Ángel García Català, Jenni Hulse, Helen Jukes, Matt Malone, Orfeo Mattar
Graphic designer Sam Hails
Cover design Brett Biedscheid
Printed by Page Bros., Norwich, UK

Volume 39 No 1 2010

Supported by
**ARTS COUNCIL
ENGLAND**

NEW FRONTIERS

Jo Glanville

In January, the Iranian government warned opposition groups that it was monitoring their emails and text messages, looking for people who might be organising protests. In the same week, Google declared that Chinese hackers had accessed Gmail and that they were reconsidering their position in China. Both incidents highlight what has become of fundamental importance for the protection of free speech today: the safeguarding of privacy.

Anyone who uses email, searches for information online or belongs to a social network is surrendering private information about themselves that is open to abuse. In her revealing interview for Index with David Drummond, Google's chief legal officer, Rebecca MacKinnon asks whether Google has taken the question of privacy seriously enough. She makes the novel suggestion that Google should start treating its users 'more like citizens of [a] place rather than users or customers. In order to gain people's trust ... does there not need to be a new kind of thinking?' Gus Hosein echoes MacKinnon's concerns in his article on political surveillance and points out that modern telecommunications systems 'are designed with backdoors to enable state surveillance. ... We need to renew our safeguards for privacy as a political right'.

Some of the world's leading authorities on technology and free speech have contributed to this special issue of Index, and their observations and insights are of concern to us all. Censorship has not died – as internet pioneers once predicted – it has been reborn. Not only does the internet make it possible for authoritarian regimes to monitor their citizens' activities as never before, it has also made censorship acceptable, and even respectable, in democracies.

Politicians and policy-makers call for filtering and blocking in the name of child protection, counter-terrorism and intellectual property. In the face of new technology, transparency and democratic accountability appear to

Internet cafe, Hefei, Anhui Province, China, 1 July 2009
Credit: Jianan Yu/Reuters

theguardian
HAY FESTIVAL
27 May–6 June 2010

ideas may blossom

Broadcast sponsor
skyARTS

www.hayfestival.com
box office 01497 822 629

have been bizarrely and dangerously abandoned. As Joe McNamee points out, blocking images of child abuse may appear to be laudable, but it has actually become a smokescreen for political failure: not only does blocking fail to stop access to such sites, it gives politicians the appearance of taking action when in fact no concrete steps are actually being made to tackle child abuse networks. It's evident that politicians are in urgent need of computer literate advisers, whose commitment to human rights and tackling crime transcends the urge to populism.

This issue also includes Index's founding editor, Michael Scammell, on the origins of the magazine; novelist and translator Maureen Freely on a day of reckoning for Turkey; an exclusive extract from playwright Gurpreet Kaur Bhatti's brilliant new satire on censorship and an interview with Italian documentary-maker Erik Gandini on his award-winning documentary *Videocracy*. You can follow our campaigns and the latest censorship news on www.indexoncensorship.org.

This is our first issue with our new publisher SAGE and we're delighted to be able to offer improved subscription rates for magazine subscribers (details inside front cover). You can also now buy Index on Amazon. It's the beginning of an exciting new era, at a time when it's never been more important to protect free speech. ❐

©Jo Glanville
39(1): 3/5
DOI: 10.1177/0306422010363075
www.indexoncensorship.org

CONTENTS

AGAINST TYRANNY

Internet cafe, Kuala Lumpur, Malaysia, August 2009
Credit: Batuki Muhammad/Reuters

DISPATCHES

Mourners carry placards reading: 'We all are Armenians' 'We all are Hrant Dink', Istanbul, 23 January 2007
Credit: Fatih Saribas/Reuters

SECRET HISTORIES

As Turkey grapples with an unprecedented string of military scandals, a new book re-examines the legacy of the Armenian genocide, reports **Maureen Freely**

The British press paid intense attention to Orhan Pamuk when he was prosecuted in 2005 for insulting Turkishness, after publicly acknowledging that a million Armenians had been killed in Anatolia in the last years of the Ottoman Empire. Though it paid considerably less attention to Hrant Dink, the Turkish-Armenian journalist who was prosecuted on similar charges by the same ultra-nationalist lawyer, there was ample coverage of Dink's assassination outside the offices of *Agos*, his newspaper, in January 2007, and also of his funeral, attended by 100,000 mourners from all religions and backgrounds, many carrying placards declaring, 'We are all Armenians, we are all Hrant Dink.'

But when – just a few days after a mass vigil marking the first anniversary of Dink's death – the government announced that it had arrested 33 members of an alleged state-sponsored terror organisation named Ergenekon (amongst them Kemal Kerinçsiz, the lawyer who initiated the prosecutions against Pamuk, Dink, and other prominent novelists, journalists, and democrats), the consensus on the foreign desk was that it was 'not a story'. That, for the most part, is the position two years on. In Turkey, meanwhile, it's called the story of the century, and it gets curiouser and curiouser every day.

Over the past 12 months, various European and American think tanks have put out weighty analyses of the Ergenekon trials (there are now three, with the first indictment running to 2,455 pages, the second to 1,909, and the third to 1,454, and the number of detentions now well into three digits). All agree that it is a very complicated story, and no one seems to know quite how to read it. There are even suggestions that Ergenekon is not a real organisation but a name invented by the prosecutors or their sponsors in the ruling party, the Islamist Justice and Development Party (AKP), so that they can prosecute their enemies, thereby bringing down the military and, with it, the secularist republic. But even those expert observers who support or actively promote this view will concede that there has long been a culture of impunity that has allowed a rogue clique located at the heart of the state to prosecute, persecute, imprison, murder and silence all groups and individuals who challenge Turkey's monolithic state ideology. Most also concede that this clique has its roots in a Gladio-type 'stay behind' group of the type established by the CIA in just about every country in Europe during the cold war. Some see its ideological origins in the Committee of Union and Progress and the Young Turks, who took the ailing empire into the First World War on the losing side and are directly implicated in the 1915 Armenian genocide.

Technically such claims can still lead to prosecution or worse. In practice, this is impossible, because the cat is out of the bag. The state-enforced taboo that kept most Turks in the dark about the events of 1915 is well and truly broken, and so, too, is the culture of impunity that has so long protected the enforcers. Though it continues to be against the law to criticise the army, the judiciary or the legacy of Atatürk, a string of scandals, each more shocking than the last, most initiated by journalists working for a new campaigning newspaper called *Taraf*, have seriously eroded public trust in the military and the court system. One involved documents, now universally accepted as genuine and emanating from a well-placed, and still anonymous, whistleblower last November, outlining detailed plans by members of the Turkish armed forces to undermine the ruling party through a series of devious and deniable strategies. The plan was to step up the harassment of the country's non-Muslim minorities, not just by gathering information on the readership of dissenting newspapers like *Agos* and *Taraf*, but also by assassinating leading members of their communities and placing bombs on the ferries serving the Princes' Islands, where many of Istanbul's non-Muslims have summer homes. These were later to be attributed to Islamist extremists, thereby killing two birds with one stone. The so-called Cage Plan, which caused huge public outrage, has since been superseded by the release of secret documents pertaining to the so called Sledgehammer Plan, which proposed extreme measures (the bombing of major mosques, the shooting down of a Turkish jet, and the rounding up of named dissidents in football stadiums) all to provoke or consolidate a coup. Many of those implicated are now under interrogation or behind bars — these include high-ranking officers on active duty as well as retired generals, admirals and air force commanders. It is an entirely unprecedented situation and no one is sure where it might lead.

How did all this begin? Many credit the EU, or rather, its accession process, which called for Turkey's army and state bureaucracies to democratise. But to leave it there would be to occlude, or at least underestimate, Turkey's democratisers – by which I mean the diverse networks – Kurdish and Alevi, Islamist and secularist, social democrat, leftist, and feminist, academic and activist, Muslim and non-Muslim – that have, in addition to fighting for legal and structural changes, mounted an ever more ambitious challenge to state ideology and the official history that sustains it. Though its concerns are as diverse as they are themselves, they agree on the importance of telling the truth about Anatolia's Armenians.

So education, or rather, re-education, is of central importance: until now, the Turkish public has largely accepted the official history because that is the only version that has ever been available to them. The adulation of Atatürk might be state-sponsored and state-enforced, but outside those areas that have suffered greatly at the hands of the military, it can also be heartfelt. How to reach those Turks whose very identity rests on their pride in Atatürk, and whose belief in his official history was cemented in primary school? And how to be heard over the din created in recent years by the republic's ultranationalist publishers, newspapers, websites, TV dramatists and film makers, who have been working overtime to provide narratives that don't just confirm the official history, but make it shinier and more seductive than ever?

One way is to suggest, through family memoirs, that Turks might not be as Turkish as they like to think. The lawyer Fethiye Çetin did just this with her memoir *My Grandmother,* in which she revealed that her maternal grandmother had confessed to her late in life that she was not a Muslim Turk but had been born Armenian, having been pulled from a death march by a police commissar who then brought her up as his own. Çetin is also the lawyer of Hrant Dink's family. The memoir was first published in 2004 – a year before Orhan Pamuk was prosecuted, when any Turk publicly acknowledging the

Lawyer and writer Fethiye Çetin talks to the media as she leaves court in Istanbul, 2 July 2007
Credit: Osman Orsal/Reuters

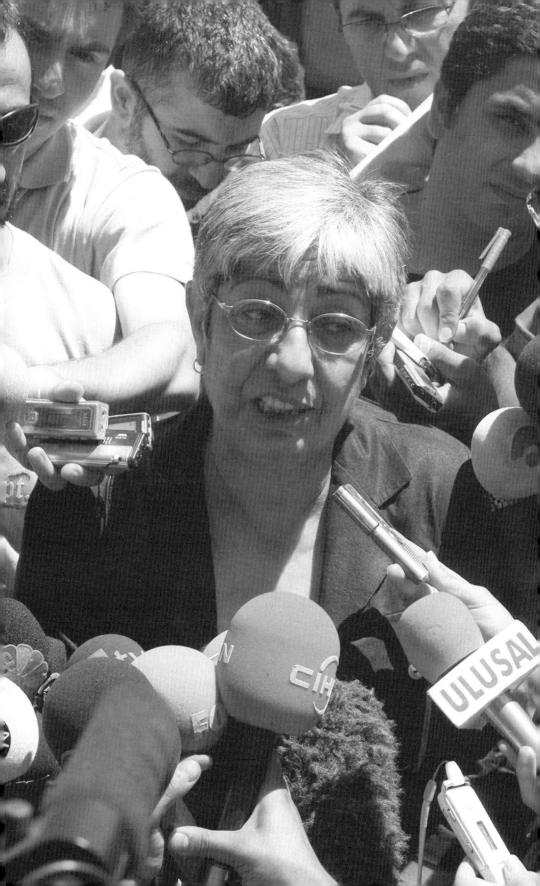

slaughter of Anatolia's Armenians in 1915 could expect ostracism, prosecution, or worse. But Çetin's account of her grandmother's true history became an immediate bestseller: it is estimated that as many as two million Turks have at least one Armenian grandparent.

It is partly thanks to *My Grandmother* that others have begun to speak about the secret Armenians in their own families. Over the past five years, Çetin and three others travelled all over Anatolia listening to their stories, and last October they published the 25 most striking interviews in *Grandchildren*. Like its predecessor, it is pushing at an open door. In its first month, it sold 4,000 copies, sparking off painful new debates about the national myths it so effectively demolishes.

Readers of *My Grandmother* are now well equipped to question what they were taught at school about Turkish identity. They know that present-day Turkey is made up of a multitude of ethnic groups, some of Asian origin and some of European, some Muslim and others non-Muslim. They know of the slaughter and displacement of peoples during the contraction of the Ottoman Empire and particularly during the turmoil of the First World War. They know that the Turk was more or less an invention of Atatürk – designed to bring to the disparate peoples of his new republic an identity of which they could be proud. But they also understand that his decision to underpin that concept with a white-washed history has been (and continues to be) hugely damaging, not just to those who have had to suppress their true origins to fit in with the state-imposed model, but also to Turkish society as a whole. They leave the book convinced that the only way forward is greater honesty.

Readers are convinced the only way forward is greater honesty

Grandchildren was conceived in much the same spirit, but its authors quickly found themselves stumbling onto disturbing new terrain. When deciding which grandchildren to include in this volume, they opted only for those who 'opened new doors' for them. Those discussing the book in the Turkish press have made much of the fact that all but two of those interviewed have chosen to use alibis.

More than half of those included identify as Kurds – or they did until they found out, usually in adulthood, that they were part Armenian. It is well known that Kurdish tribes were encouraged and possibly paid to slaughter their Armenian neighbours in 1915, and that many did so believing that they would be rewarded with their own homeland. By and large they killed the men of fighting age, dispatching the rest – the women and children, the elderly and the infirm – on death marches. Some children were 'saved' along the way by kindly or well-rewarded neighbours. But many of the grandmothers and great-grandmothers remembered in this volume were women not saved but abducted. Forcibly converted to Islam, and forcibly married, they often entered Kurdish households as second wives. Robbed of their identity, their language and their religion, they nevertheless found other ways to assert themselves. Cleanliness continued to equal godliness. Unwilling converts sometimes found in Islam another way to God. Many put huge effort into encouraging children and grandchildren – both male and female – into bettering their lives through education. Some refused to defer to their husbands. However they behaved, most endured a lifetime of domestic violence – and had no choice but to endure it in silence.

So the grandchildren's testimony forces readers to acknowledge that 1915 is not just about the Armenians but about the Kurds, not just about the histories and religions that divide them but about the patriarchal practices they share. As Çetin's co-author Ayşegül Altınay points out in her hard-hitting afterword, even the best scholars of the Armenian diaspora have colluded with the genocide denialists of the Turkish state in writing off 'those left behind'. Once these women entered Muslim society, they ceased to be counted as Armenians by either camp. And yet they could still pass on the stigma. This book is full of shocking accounts of the social ostracism and state-sponsored discrimination suffered even today by the children, grandchildren and even great-grandchildren of Anatolia's 'converts'.

But the most haunting accounts are by those whose families somehow managed to cut the cord. One witness speaks of growing up in an Anatolian town with his mother, his father, and an 'aunt who was not a blood relation'. It later emerged that the three were all children from the same Armenian village. They lived in perpetual fear of being 'found out'. Another witness speaks of his shock upon going into the military and being told that he was good for nothing, on account of being descended from a convert. The 'mark' remained on his record, and when he returned to civilian life he continued to be barred from certain kinds of work. That this form of discrimination still continues is confirmed by a civil servant who now knows of his own Armenian ancestry. When he thinks what might happen if it became knowledge amongst his colleagues, he goes into 'a cold sweat'. Yet another witness speaks of growing up in a village that, though claiming to be Alevi, never followed the practices of that branch of Islam. Instead they had feasts at Christmas and Easter that were devoid of religious content. From time to time, villagers were given to wondering 'what they really were'. They may have converted (by force or choice) to Islam at a politically dangerous moment prior to 1915. They may not have been Armenian but Assyrian Christians (who were also slaughtered in large numbers) or Yezidis. The grandchild witness remembers sitting in the hills with an elderly relative who spoke of the Armenian villages that had once surrounded theirs. 'We didn't take anything from their houses,' he said, 'but we didn't protect them.' Pointing at the Tigris, he said, 'They threw them all in there.'

This is the sort of history that readers of *Grandchildren* are now being asked to own. In the words of one witness, 'all those who colluded in this long silence are to blame'. To the silencing state and its silenced citizens we now need to add the silence of the Kurds, the silence of the Armenian diaspora, and the (until now) almost universal reluctance to acknowledge the sexual repression suffered not just by 'those left behind' but by all women in the households they were forced to join.

Grandchildren has already attracted attention amongst the international network of scholars, journalists, writers and human activists now conversing electronically about history and politics in the post-Ottoman world. They are already preparing for the arguments that will follow its publication in French and English. Meanwhile, back in Turkey, we see a nation unlearning the myths of nationhood, while its many peoples struggle to understand who they really are. ❐

©Maureen Freely
39(1): 14/20
DOI: 10.1177/0306422010362178
www.indexoncensorship.org

Maureen Freely is a writer, translator and senior lecturer at Warwick University. *Grandchildren*, by Ayşegül Altınay and Fethiye Çetin, is published by Metis, Istanbul. Her latest novel, *Enlightenment*, is published by Marion Boyars

Casting for television showgirls, from Erik Gandini's film Videocracy, 2009
Credit: Atmo, www.atmo.se

TELEVISION PREMIER

Documentary maker **Erik Gandini** tells Giulio D'Eramo
why appearance matters more than truth in Italy

Erik Gandini is the acclaimed documentary maker of Surplus: Terrorised into Being Consumers *and* Sacrificio: Who Betrayed Che Guevara. *He was born in northern Italy and now lives in Sweden. His new documentary* Videocracy *is a critical portrait of the Italian broadcast media and its impact on the country's culture. The film's release last year coincided with embarrassing revelations about Berlusconi's romantic escapades and went on to win the Toronto film festival award for best documentary and the special jury award at the Sheffield film festival. It has also been a surprise hit at the Italian box office.*

Videocracy *is an overview of the past 30 years of Italian television, start-ing with the 1976 local television show* Spogliamoci insieme *(Let's undress together), which was an instant hit and inspired some of Berlusconi's Mediaset blockbusters of the following decades. Through exclusive interviews with prominent media figures in the country, as well as wannabe media stars, the documentary paints a dark picture of the superficial, discriminating and cyni-cal nature of the television world and its impact on politics. It explores what is known as the Italian anomaly – the political monopoly of the broadcast media in a western democracy. Thirty years of being bombarded with images of a world where girls dance semi-naked all day long and everybody is happy, smiling and beautiful have taken their toll on the political landscape in Italy. With the unpleasant knowledge that what has happened in Italy could hap-pen elsewhere,* Videocracy *serves as a cautionary tale, as well as a chilling account of Italian contemporary history.*

Giulio D'Eramo: Is the documentary an attack on Berlusconi or on the mono-lithic media structure?

Erik Gandini: When I make a movie I never do it against something or some-body. As a director, I usually try to turn an abstract idea into a story, not in a journalistic way but as a visual description of a real situation, to allow viewers to experience it first hand. In the case of *Videocracy* there are a few interconnecting ideas that I wanted to represent, namely the overwhelming power of television in Italy and the culture that it transmits. So *Videocracy* tells the story of what lies behind the shiny culture of Italian television, where words are constantly defeated by images and impressions. I show what Silvio [Berlusconi] would never show: the cynical and greedy backstage of his TV world, in which everybody is happy and girls dance naked all day long.

That the movie that came out of this was in many aspects terrifying – some American critics called it the best horror movie of the year – is only due to the reality I represent. To answer the question – the documentary is an attack on the idea that everything is just fine, that we need to enjoy ourselves in a sort of self-motivating hedonism, and an attack on the frightening moral decadence that this concept implies.

Giulio D'Eramo: If we watch the main national TV channels we can see that Rai state television offers exactly the same content as Berlusconi's channels. Should we then assume that it is the Italian public that represents an anomaly and not the media itself?

Erik Gandini: The aim of a public service is that of improving society. The idea of a television that educates, stimulates and is without commercials is very strong in Sweden, but also in the UK, where the BBC keeps offering a unique service. In those, and in many other countries, television can be seen as a window on the world: from your home. You can get a picture of what happens on the other side of the world or in places you would never visit. It is worth observing that Italian state television is by law obliged to follow these same principles, even though it obviously does not do so. Another defeat for words.

One more thing: investigative television programmes usually lead to the start of an official investigation, often resulting in a trial, and eventually a sentence for the guilty. In Italy, instead, they are just labelled as political journalism, be it left or right leaning, and therefore disregarded as just opinion. The very idea of a journalistic truth as an undeniable truth, a sort of contract according to which the viewer watches the show and the presenter tells the truth, has long disappeared in Italy. Whatever the evidence, be it about Berlusconi's prostitutes, his financial misdemeanours or the corruption scandals of leftist politicians, it is now presented as an opinion. In Italy the truth is no more, there only exists opinion.

Giulio D'Eramo: Where do you think the responsibility lies?

Erik Gandini: In Italy, there are enormous responsibilities held by a lot of people, including all the Rai journalists who have long accepted the disruption to their working ethics and their values. Those values are something that everyone has to safeguard, not only those in charge.

Giulio D'Eramo: Where does Berlusconi stand in all this? Has his presence made any difference?

Erik Gandini: Television as Berlusconi is trying to keep it, by means of political pressure or straightforward censorship, is a television that does not discuss the important events. It does not let you travel around the world, but only through Berlusconi's vision. What his television brings forward is an amoral morality, a system in which the only virtue is to be ruthless. The values it carries are egoism, money, appearance, individual success. This is a very high price to pay to get some entertainment.

When Berlusconi entered the political arena, many people voted for him thinking that he would do for Italy what he did for his own companies, attracted by the legend of a man that turns everything into gold. What they got from their vote is instead the introduction of his pervasive, cynical and discriminatory commercial TV culture at all levels of society. This is what he brought: TV models turned into ministers, his professional escort girls running for the European Parliament, the equivalent of sex for a role in a movie. I would say that as Iran is an Islamic republic, Italy is now a TV republic.

Giulio D'Eramo: Some define it as 'the Italian anomaly'. Should this movie be a warning only to Italians?

Erik Gandini: The culture of banality is a global phenomenon. Italy is a clear example of the risks inherent in this culture. The evil of banality is just the evolution of a much older concept: the banality of evil.

This culture presents itself as harmless, a form of entertainment apparently risk free, but it is instead very dangerous, as we can clearly see by looking at Italy. As I said, the problem should not be limited to Berlusconi as a person, even though with him banality became total and harmful, especially concerning women. This is going to be his greatest legacy to the country when he is no longer there. The problem of 'Berlusconism', which in my opinion is a new form of totalitarianism, is that it is so new that we have a hard time defining it. Nonetheless it exists, and not only in Italy.

Giulio D'Eramo: Are there any factors specific to Italy that could have helped Berlusconi achieve his entrepreneurial success as a media tycoon?

Erik Gandini: Berlusconi started to emerge as a media tycoon in the late 1970s, when Italy was going through a period of violent daily confrontations between the extreme left and the extreme right that led to hundreds of deaths.

A few months ago, at a conference on the state of the Italian media, I met Pino Maffi, the presenter of the 1976 show *Spogliamoci insieme* (Let's undress together), broadcast from a Turin-based local TV channel that was later bought by Berlusconi. It's the show featured in the trailer of *Videocracy* and is very similar to the 1980s Fininvest commercial hit *Colpo Grosso* [a late-night entertainment show with semi-clad women], in fact they also had the same sponsor. Pino Maffi, who started off by excusing himself for the monster he unintentionally helped to create, said that at that time the situation was very tense, there were a lot of political kidnappings and bombings, so that people really needed a way to escape all this. The aim of his show was to entertain the public (and especially the Turin factory workers, dangerously exposed to the charm of political activism) by showing them a shiny world that did not exist.

One more thing to consider is the presence of the Vatican, which surely did help Berlusconi. In fact, due to its influence, Rai TV was not only forbidden from featuring lightly dressed women, but also from advertising some products, as was the case for dog food (do not ask me why that was the case, I don't know). Berlusconi managed to profit from those weaknesses. We all remember that the Mediaset channels hosted a lot of pet food advertisements. He proposed something that nobody else was able to offer, just as when he entered politics offering an anti-political party right after the end of the cold war.

Giulio D'Eramo: Did you learn anything from making this movie?

Erik Gandini: Only after the movie was complete did I understand what *Videocracy* was really about: the power of images. Berlusconi is at the same time the most powerful and the richest man in Italy, but he has succeeded in portraying himself as a victim. Why? Because he manages to transmit the impression that he is a victim. There again there is a truth, and the truth is that he is not a victim. It is a clear example that in certain circumstances, as for Italy in the past 15 years, images matter more than facts, and appearances more than the truth. This is kind of a philosophical problem: if, as a powerful man, you can shape the truth as you wish, then there is no need for censorship.

This new wave of censorship is new for Berlusconi – a media tycoon who understood how to shape the reality to his own liking – and almost anachronistic. In fact, it is Berlusconi himself who showed the world how censorship is an outdated instrument, old and useless, by effectively convincing so many Italians of a reality that should only be in his dreams. ❐

© Giulio D'Eramo
39(1): 22/26
DOI: 10.1177/0306422010362180
www.indexoncensorship.org

Giulio D'Eramo writes for *Index on Censorship* and *Red Pepper*

E-resources now available from SAGE

Photography© Edmund Sumner 2006

AGE Premier - access to 480+ SAGE journal titles in 2008 via SAGE Journals Online.

AGE Deep Backfile – Coverage back to Volume 1, Issue 1.
ease and purchase options available for individual libraries and library consortia.

AGE Full-Text Collections - ten popular discipline-specific databases.

AGE eReference - authoritative and award-winning encyclopedias now available online:
ww.sage-ereference.com

EW Primary Sources in Counselling and Psychology: 1950 to Present - An Online
atabase of Transcripts, Primary Accounts, and Handbooks and Reference Works from
exander Street Press and SAGE. For more information visit www.alexanderstreetpress.
om/products/psyc.htm

r more information on any of the above, please contact **journalsales@sagepub.co.uk**

ww.**sagepub.co.uk**

BRAVE NEW WORDS

The good, the bad and the ugly:
what technology did for free speech

Testing cyber devices at a computer fair, Hanover, Germany, 17 March 2007
Credit: Hannibal Hanschke/Reuters

GOOGLE RULES

Rebecca MacKinnon talks to **David Drummond** about privacy, censorship and China

Ever since Google entered China in 2006 and launched a censored Chinese search engine, Google.cn, the company has come under fire from human rights groups and free speech activists for helping to legitimise the Chinese government's censorship policies. Staffers say that Google's decision to comply with Chinese censorship in order to enter China's fast-growing and potentially lucrative market was made only after heated internal debates over the ethical pros and cons.

In January 2006, at the time of Google.cn's launch, senior policy counsel Andrew McLaughlin explained that his company was trying to remain true to the company mantra, 'don't be evil'. He acknowledged that censoring Google.cn's search results 'clearly compromises our mission', but he argued that 'failing to offer Google search at all to a fifth of the world's population, however, does so far more severely'. McLaughlin also made clear that while Google was going into China with censored search, it would be keeping other services like Gmail and blogspot out of China in order to avoid making further compromises on user privacy and freedom of expression.

On 15 December 2009, I interviewed David Drummond, Google's senior vice president, corporate development and chief legal officer, at the company's idyllic campus-like headquarters known as the 'Googleplex' in Mountain View, California. By bizarre coincidence, at the same time a massive, highly sophisticated attack was launched from China against Google's systems. The attackers honed in on Gmail and, even more specifically, the accounts of human rights activists who work on China issues. The attack lasted into early January. On 12 January, David Drummond announced on the official Google Policy Blog that his company was rethinking its business in China:

> *These attacks and the surveillance they have uncovered – combined with the attempts over the past year to further limit free speech on the web – have led us to conclude that we should review the feasibility of our business operations in China. We have decided we are no longer willing to continue censoring our results on Google. cn, and so over the next few weeks we will be discussing with the Chinese government the basis on which we could operate an unfiltered search engine within the law, if at all. We recognise that this may well mean having to shut down Google.cn, and potentially our offices in China.*

Soon after the announcement, I emailed David Drummond some follow-up questions. As this issue goes to press, the fallout over Google's public stand against Chinese censorship and attacks aimed at obtaining the private communications of Google's users continues. Below is an edited transcript: the more recent emailed questions appear on pages 35–36 followed by the December interview.

Our conversation dealt not only with China. At the time of the interview, Drummond and three other Google executives were facing criminal charges in Italy over a video of an autistic child being bullied by classmates: in late February, an Italian judge found Drummond and two of the other executives guilty of privacy invasion. Google intends to appeal the six-month suspended sentences, calling the ruling an attack on 'the very principles of freedom on which the internet is built'. RM

Rebecca MacKinnon: When we spoke on 15 December, you defended Google's decision to be in China. Was Google management already starting to reconsider things at that time? Or did it all happen after the most recent round of hacker attacks – which I understand started right around the time we did the interview?

David Drummond: We discovered in December that Google had been the target of an unusually sophisticated cyber attack. When we launched Google.cn in 2006, we believed that the benefits of increased access to information in China for Chinese citizens and a more open internet outweighed the discomfort of agreeing to censor some results. While many of these arguments still hold true, we believe the events of the last year mean we can no longer, in all good conscience, continue to co-operate with the Chinese authorities in filtering results on Google.cn.

As we said when we launched Google.cn in January 2006, 'We will carefully monitor conditions in China, including new laws and other restrictions on our services. If we determine that we are unable to achieve the objectives outlined we will not hesitate to reconsider our approach to China.'

Rebecca MacKinnon: To what degree was the decision to re-evaluate Google's presence in China about the hacker attack [in January], to what degree was it about the worsening censorship environment, and to what degree was it about other – more pragmatic – short and long-term commercial considerations, both in China as well as globally? If you had to apply a percentage weighting to each factor what would it be?

David Drummond: What's clear is that the environment in which we were operating in terms of an open internet was not improving in China. There have been a number of episodes over the past year that have widely been reported on, including the events surrounding Green Dam content-control software, as well as people in China reporting difficulties in accessing services from Google and other internet companies, as well as the blockage of YouTube. That, combined with these attacks and the surveillance they have uncovered, meant we decided to take a new approach in China.

In terms of commercial considerations – we just had our most successful quarter ever in China, but our revenues there are not material to our business, and a large percentage of them are for the export market – that is, Chinese companies advertising to users abroad on our different search engines. This decision was about freedom of expression and an open internet.

Rebecca MacKinnon: A lot of internet users in China were very upset upon first hearing Google might leave. They are worried the Chinese internet will become more closed and balkanised than ever before. What's your message to them?

David Drummond: We hope to find a solution with the Chinese government. Our Chinese users, partners and employees are very important to us, and we hope we can find a positive outcome. We hope to be able to operate securely in China and in a way that increases access to information for our users in China. We will be discussing with the Chinese government the basis on which we could operate an unfiltered search engine within the law, if at all. But we recognise that this may mean having to shut down Google.cn, and potentially our offices in China. We are committed to protecting the safety and security of our users and products and believe reviewing the feasibility of our business operations in China is the most constructive way to do that.

Rebecca MacKinnon: Do you plan to do more than you've done in the past to help Chinese internet users who want to access all the information available on the global internet – not just the sub-set of information their government wants them to see?

David Drummond: We will be meeting with the Chinese government and hope to find a mutually agreeable resolution, so it's too early to speculate. We are continuing to operate Google.cn in compliance with Chinese law, and users are also able to access our Chinese-language service on Google.com.

Rebecca MacKinnon: Are you disappointed that other companies seem disinclined to follow Google's lead?

David Drummond: We're not going to comment on specific companies. As we have made clear, at least 20 other large companies from a wide range of businesses – including the internet, finance, technology, media and chemical sectors – have been similarly targeted.

Undemocratic trends (December interview)
Rebecca MacKinnon: Google went through a lot of soul searching in making the decision to go into China – to do it with google.cn, but not to move forward with other services like Gmail or blogger. But even so, might one argue that this one compromise started Google down a slippery slope that

has made government censorship demands of international internet companies more legitimate? Or has helped to legitimise the compliance with government censorship requests in a global way? And has it also made it more possible for other governments – from Thailand to Turkey to Italy – to expect that Google will comply with demands to take down content, remove results, filter certain content?

David Drummond: No. I don't think that's true. No, not at all. We've been quite clear that what we did with China was something we did specifically in China because of the specific dynamics that are in that market and in that country, which is a unique country on the face of the earth. There is no question about that.

I don't believe that anything we did in China had any effect on the Thai government's requests of us, the Turkish government's requests of us, the Italian government's requests of us, on any state government's or state police's requests on us at all. Nor did what we did in China have any effect on our responses – we have stood firm against lots of requests. We've honoured them where we felt they were legitimate, but not where they weren't. That has not changed, and I don't think China, and our decision to enter China in the way that we did, had any effect on that. As for other internet companies, I don't think that what we did should have any impact on them either – it's up to them how they operate.

Rebecca MacKinnon: When we think about chilling effects on free expression we tend to pick China, we tend to think of Iran, but are you concerned that there are trends in democratic nations that are going to make it harder for Google to be a platform of free expression?

David Drummond: Over the past couple of years, the focus of issues around censorship and free expression has almost moved from non-democratic states like China or Vietnam to emerging democracies or emerging economies. Places like Thailand or Turkey. Now, more and more, we are seeing rumblings in what seem to be democratic countries. Let me give you an example: South Korea, where they passed a law saying you had to identify yourself if you post anything – with your real identity, through the use of a national ID number. It's hugely chilling to free speech. In France, apparently, there are legislators talking about the same thing now. In Australia, the government has passed this law that allows a blacklist of terms and sites that the government will be empowered to censor. All in the name of

Computer class, Istanbul, Turkey, 16 April 2008
Credit: Osman Orsal/Reuters

filtering and child protection. But when you heard the conservative govern-ment down there talking about it, it was clear they had designs perhaps on things that were offensive to Christianity and on harmful content beyond child protection.

And that is where it seems to start in the West – protecting children. Everybody agrees child pornography is illegal and all of us should do some-thing about it, but protecting children and then moving forward from there does seem like the slippery slope unless we start turning things around.

Rebecca MacKinnon: So speaking of trying to get it turned around and what Google may be doing on that – I understand that [last December] Google hosted a meeting which was written about on the Google policy blog. Some people from the Citizen Lab in Toronto and the Open Net Initiative came, and basically gave a presentation on the fact that filtering, the blocking of web-sites at a national level, is growing all over the world, just as you describe.

And on this blog, a colleague of yours wrote that given the urgency of this issue [Google is] hoping to bring online free expression to the forefront of policy discussions. So I'm wondering if you could elaborate a bit on how Google plans to do this.

David Drummond: We think that too often the problems of censorship on the internet have been made out to be issues solely between a repressive government and some internet actor or some internet company – and those were the only players you had to be concerned about. The fact of the matter is that it's a government to government issue. We have been trying to engage governments in the West who care about this issue and get them to start raising this question and use their powers of persuasion on other governments, who perhaps don't have the free speech traditions, and put pressure on them to maintain an open and free internet.

Censorship is bad for business

I think that holding governments' feet to the fire on the principle [of human rights] is something we'd like to do. Now, we also realise that getting governments to implement human rights treaties has not exactly been … there are not a lot of great examples of universal success there. So the other angle we are taking is encouraging western governments – and we have talked to the US government quite a bit about this – to make free expression a trade issue. Because indeed it is, right? If you are talking about the internet – in addition to being a global means of expression it is a global means of trade.

For a country like, say, China to use filtering and censorship in order to make it difficult for companies from other places to operate – it seems like that ought to be addressed. When you are talking about multilateral or bilateral trade discussions, just as piracy has been put on the agenda, free expression should be put on the agenda. It ought to be something that is part of the conversation, and western governments whose economies certainly benefit from the hi-tech sector, the internet sector, [should] make this happen.

Rebecca MacKinnon: How much success are you having so far? Particularly with the US government?

David Drummond: The US government has been receptive, there have been a number of conversations with the State Department and the trade representative's office and I think they're very interested in this idea. Same with the UK government.

A question of transparency

Rebecca MacKinnon: I'm on a list with a whole other bunch of observers – activists – who are working against censorship in various countries. One person on the list actually just complained that they feel that Google is not transparent enough with users about what it is doing in Thailand – the filtering of specific content and so on. It may be clear to Google and to the Thai government – or to insiders – what is going on, but it is completely unclear to users on the ground why certain things are blocked and why certain other things are not blocked. Could Google perhaps be doing a better job at helping users understand what's going on here?

David Drummond: Probably. Yes, we probably could. And that is something I certainly think we should strive to do better on. I think one of the best ways to fight censorship is to shed light when it happens. I think it is pretty important for us to make clear to our users and to the world when it is that we feel required to remove something.

Rebecca MacKinnon: When you are delisting search results, you have this thing that says some results have been removed, but it doesn't end up solving the problem. You are helping to create an environment where people's information environment is manipulated and they don't know what they don't know – because it has been delisted they have no way of figuring out what information it is that they are being denied. Of course, that is the point of censorship, and which you continue to enable – even though you've got the warning sign, even though people are seeing that they are not getting the results. So, how do you respond to that? How might Google help make it more clear to users, how they can go about discovering what it is they are being deprived of?

David Drummond: Google.com is always going to be unfiltered, and so it is up to governments to block that if they want to – some of them do. If we are in a position where we feel we have to comply with the law – I mean it is very easy for an activist just to say, 'You shouldn't be there', but the fact of the matter is it's important for us to be in some of these countries.

We are in a position where we are trying to deliver internet services and tools to people which change their lives and make their lives better, and there are times when we can't do that. We can do that and risk our employees going to jail and risk further blockages and so forth. But you've got to decide where it's just an obvious end run on the law, and then it's tough for us. Which is why, again, we think a lot more activism should be directed towards getting these governments to change some laws. Especially when you are talking about governments that western governments trade with, have diplomatic relations with. We are not just talking about rogue governments here. And so that was my point earlier, that we should be ratcheting up the pressure on these governments that want to do business with the West, that want help from the West, that want to deal with the West.

Focusing on internet companies only, which has tended to be what happens in this debate, or this discussion, I think doesn't help. There is only so much an internet company can do. The choices are: you stay there, push back, insist that if someone's going to try and get information from you, or get you to censor something, that they are following a law. And you make sure that you think that the law was legitimate, in the sense that there is some form of democratic process that created it. You go through all of that, with a very, very narrow view for what you are going to do here. You make these calls that sometimes someone's not going to agree with, but the alternative is: you're not there at all.

Rebecca MacKinnon: And then people have even less access. I'm going to push a little bit more on that, however, understanding that this is tough, these are tough decisions, and that they are made by people who are trying to do the right thing. Nonetheless, by complying with censorship demands at all, and in the short term enabling people to access your services, which very arguably does those people a lot of good, however, does that also lessen the pressure and lessen the urgency for people to engage in the kind of activism that you are advocating: activism directed against the government to change their policies? Does it make people less urgent about it because they are getting enough of Google? Whereas if you guys just didn't compromise at all, and got blocked pretty much everywhere, would there be so much anger from so many people that that would actually – in the more medium term – lead to more pressure for governments to change their policies and not to filter?

David Drummond: No, that just doesn't work, because the predominant mode that we operate in is we push back and we don't censor, right? And that has led to lots of blockages. And in some cases blocks have caused internet users to hue and cry and in some countries caused governments to lift blocks – certainly that has happened. But look, China is what we are really talking about here. And I think it is a nice theoretical point to make. But if [we're talking about] the realities of providing internet services on the ground to people and what they actually get out of them, I think that practically speaking it is a better course to try to navigate it as best you can.

Rebecca MacKinnon and David Drummond

Keeping it private

Rebecca MacKinnon: [Google chief executive] Eric Schmidt of course created a lot of uproar [at the end of last year] with his comments that 'If you have something you don't want anyone to know then maybe you shouldn't be doing it in the first place', and people felt that this is a bit dismissive about privacy. What would you have to say to them to reassure them that Google takes their privacy seriously?

David Drummond: Well, we'll say what we always say – which is that we lead the industry in the things that we do to protect people's privacy. I defy you to point to an instance in which we have damaged someone's privacy or we've caused harm because of the way we operate with information. If you look at the way we built our products and the things we say about that shows that there is a strong commitment there. We have to. If we didn't we really wouldn't have much of a business. If users truly believed that we weren't protecting their privacy they wouldn't use the services, because they don't have to.

The power of Google

Rebecca MacKinnon: Despite what you say about Google having all the best intentions on privacy and really working on it, Google has a reputation problem in that there is a public perception that Google has too much power, has too much of our information.

David Drummond: Some people have that perception, but I'd say that millions and millions of our users don't.

Rebecca MacKinnon: Different people have different perceptions. But we all depend on Google's products for a lot of things. This is in part because the products are very good – I'm a Gmail user and so on. But at the same time you do have this huge responsibility and – of course – Google has the mantra 'don't be evil', and you are a member of Global Network Initiative [forum of NGOs and industry advancing freedom of expression in technology]. You are doing various things to try and prove to users that 'Look, we really do have your best interests in mind.'

Yet there are still a lot of people who don't buy that necessarily. Even though they might still be using Google products, just because they are so ubiquitous. Google is in uncharted territory, in so many different ways, in our society today, and Google is part of this layer that is being built – information, web, telecommunication services, especially now you guys are getting into DNS and phones. You are building this layer upon which we depend for our personal lives and our business, our politics, everything.

While your intentions may be honourable, it turns into a whole issue of governance, really, in that this is not just a product or just even a service – it is a place. And so, do you need to start treating your users almost more like citizens of the place rather than as users or customers? In order to gain people's trust, in terms of how you make decisions, in terms of how you're approaching and shaping this layer upon which we are increasingly dependent, does there need to be a new kind of thinking?

David Drummond: We do actually do that because people vote with their feet when they use our services. They don't have to. I would quarrel with the premise that somehow Google services are the only services out there that people are using.

Rebecca MacKinnon: I'm not saying they are the only ones.

David Drummond: People use them because they work pretty well, and they don't think we are doing nefarious things with such information as they give us. I think we do have a responsibility – we carry it out. The question you have to ask yourself is: should a company like Google not innovate because of some of these concerns that have never come into play, that have never happened? And should you stop innovating, and stop doing things that users are going to really like? So in other words, if you look at things like intraspace advertising, or something like that, you say: well, you can create really useful apps, that are a lot better than apps that people see now, right? And advertisers find it really useful, and users too, because advertising is a form of information on what someone might want in a search query. An ad might even be better information than some editorial or organic kind of information.

So, should you not do it? Or should you do it in a way that tries to build in some protection, tries to build in transparency and tells people what is going on. That is what we try to do. Too many of the criticisms seem to not try to strike the balance. We are all for putting our heads together with other people and rolling up our sleeves and figuring out how we create some pretty good balances, so we don't stop innovation and create things that work really well for people, but still protect privacy. So people sense that bad things are not going to happen. We recognise that because we have got bigger and we have influence, and lots of people use our services and like using our services, that there are concerns about what we might do if we wanted to do bad things.

Rebecca MacKinnon: Like with Google Book Search. You are so much the first mover that you might turn into the world's library and nobody else will be able to duplicate it. And then there are all of these privacy issues and so on.

David Drummond: OK, there are lots of theoretical issues about what could happen, but the question is what we should then do about it. Should we not do it? Should we stop digitising books? Should we do it in a way that makes it hard to digitise books? You know, what should we do? They are complicated questions and I think, though, you've got to go back to this question of balance and make sure you are balancing innovation with these privacy concerns. And you have to go back to the question of harm and the incentives that we have. The deterrent effect is so significant, so strong – with Google – of doing anything bad, we simply wouldn't have a business or anything. I think that part is just overlooked.

Rebecca MacKinnon: I get everything you are saying. Yet it seems that Google's default is still a bit in the direction of: 'Trust us, we're good people, we're working in your interests.'

David Drummond: That is correct.

Rebecca MacKinnon: And the question is: does that work sufficiently? What are the safeguards in place to make sure that Google's power is not abused? And, of course, in American democracy we've put safeguards in place. We kind of assume that human nature is corruptible. Is Google doing enough to assume that human nature is corruptible?

David Drummond: I think we do a lot, we build things into our products that we are not required to. I think we often go above and beyond – and spend a lot of time on the privacy implications of our products and how users are affected by our products and so forth.

We're not against rules. Regulation of services likes ours exists – and exists for very good reasons. We are not opposed to privacy laws: they are very important. We follow them and we do things where we don't even have to. Intraspace advertising: there is no law that dictates we did what we did, but we did it anyway. We often go above and beyond.

In some cases legislators are grappling with how [the internet] works and whether things ought to be changed. We are a part of all of these conversations, and for a lot of these conversations it makes sense for us to be a part of them. But again, these are conversations that need to be had in terms of looking at the entire industry and looking at how it ought to develop from a current public policy standpoint, as opposed to one company that should be doing X, Y and Z. It should be what everybody should be doing, right?

Rebecca MacKinnon: Fair enough. ❐

© Rebecca MacKinnon
39(1): 32/45
DOI: 10.1177/0306422010363343
www.indexoncensorship.org

Rebecca MacKinnon is a visiting fellow at Princeton University's Center for Information Technology Policy. A former China-based journalist and academic, she is currently writing a book about the future of freedom in the internet age. She is co-founder of Global Voices Online (http://globalvoicesonline.org), a non-profit citizen media network whose many corporate and philanthropic funders include Google. Along with Google, she is also a participant in the Global Network Initiative (http://globalnetworkinitiative.org). MacKinnon receives no compensation – monetary or otherwise – for her volunteer work on both projects

Subscribe to ER
1 year: 10 issues: £25

LORDS OF MISRULE

The face of China's internet reflects the political system – repressive and chaotic, says **Xiao Shu**. Big brother is everywhere

To really understand where the Chinese internet is going, you need to understand where Chinese politics are going. To quote an advertising slogan from the *Southern Weekend*, one of China's leading newspapers, you need to be able to read China.

So what are the trends in Chinese politics today? My first generalisation would be 'restrictive' – it always has been, only it's getting more so. Many feel, when looking back over the past three decades, that each new generation of Chinese leaders has failed to match its predecessors. That former president Jiang Zemin was no Deng Xiaoping is a given; but now President Hu Jintao and Premier Wen Jiabao – for whom so many intellectuals held out so much hope – seem to have become the butt of jokes and to fail to live up to Jiang Zemin's standards. One-time critics of Jiang have even started to reminisce about that time – it seems he was more tolerant and enlightened.

I find these judgments not without foundation, but a little too easy. I agree, of course, that the political set-up has been tightening since the 1990s – but not that this is directly related to the personal qualities or preferences of our supreme rulers. I don't believe the situation is becoming more

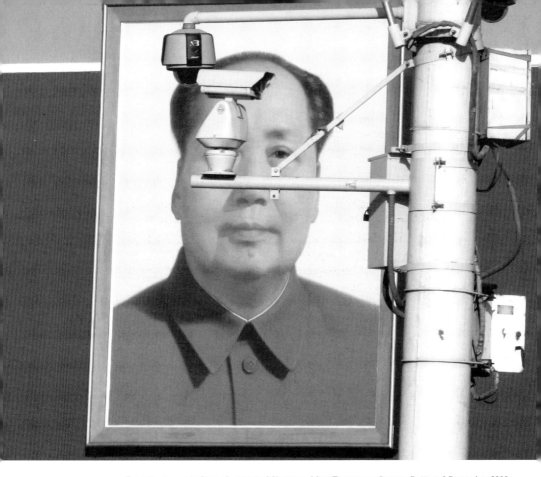

Security camera in front of portrait of Chairman Mao, Tiananmen Square, Beijing, 2 December 2009
Credit: David Gray/Reuters

restrictive because Hu and Wen are more hardline, more conservative or less able – I prefer to say that circumstances are forcing their hand.

The fundamental reason I say this is that China's political system is a game of pass the parcel – played with a firecracker set to explode. Fearing it will blow itself up, each generation of leaders dodges the real issues and passes them on to the next. Inevitably the issues worsen, while the ability and confidence to withstand and resolve social unrest and other threats weaken.

Over time, those in power come to feel isolated and under siege, and a constant squeeze on public debate – particularly online – is therefore inevitable. The restrictions around the Olympics were felt by all, but at the same time there was some hope that this was a special event, and that things would relax afterwards. But that hope was ultimately left unfulfilled. Similarly, the restrictions in the run-up to China's 60th anniversary celebrations had an impact across the country, but again there was hope – this was a special event, things would be better afterwards. But that expectation has also been left unfulfilled. The severity of the latest online crackdowns – particularly on debate – is almost unprecedented. Government jitters over an increasingly tense political situation and the greater demands of maintaining stability mean tightening up is now the norm, regardless of any imminent special events – reasons are no longer necessary. So it may be that Hu and Wen are no more hardline or conservative, or less able, than Jiang – they just don't have his luck. Jiang drew down all the political dividends of the prior three decades, bequeathing little but a shambles to Hu and Wen. They simply cannot afford the apparent tolerance and style of Jiang – when you find yourself on thin ice, caution is the only option.

My second analysis of China's political situation would be 'disorderly'. Not social disorder: this is increasing and minor incidents are common, but basic public order is easily maintained and there is no possibility of major unrest unless a grave economic crisis results in the loss of livelihoods. Even that would be offset by a robust and deeply-rooted underground and grey economy which will continue to put food on tables – and as long as there is food on tables, public order will not be affected. The seeds of unrest lie not among the people, but within the system itself, in different interest groups and in their divisions, alliances and power struggles. This will become more apparent in the future. These groups are much less able to cope with an economic crisis. If their economy collapses, they have no underground alternative to fall back on. Currently there may be a peaceable division of the spoils, but if their sources of wealth disappeared a zero-sum battle for resources would soon break out. At that point there will be no need for the people to cause unrest – it will appear within the system itself.

The foundations for this are already laid, in a de facto system of individually-held power. For many years, government orders have been said to travel no further than the gates of Zhongnanhai, the complex of Party and government offices, but now more than ever that so-called highly centralised power exists only in name. Different groups have their own different interests, as do central government, provincial governments and city governments. Even PetroChina and Sinopec – both independent commercial operations, both in the oil business and backed by government machinery – have different interests. The traditional political logic of obedience to superiors and Party central has been shattered and is now a mere formality. Multiple centres of power already exist: independent fiefdoms, closed, homogeneous and centred around powerful individuals. Each pursues the maximisation of their interests and minimisation of their responsibilities. The preservation of unity has long been a straightforward mutually beneficial exchange, not a political ideal or article of faith.

The Party talks of self-regulation: 'The Party must manage the Party.' But can it? The Party is no longer a whole, but dismembered into any number of units. Each centre of power is a Party unto itself, and that fragmentation of power cannot be halted. The process is characterised by the increasing strength and arrogance of local and departmental power-holders, and a weakening central power unable to rein them in.

And this leads directly to the situation we see on the Chinese internet. These de facto hidden regimes subject online debate to oversight not just from one source, but from many. Any level of government – even village government – can issue decrees on public debate, particularly online debate, and mobilise state violence to halt discussions that harm its own interests as soon as they start. Hence we see cases of county or city heads detaining critics even across provincial borders.

So a chaotic political situation creates an online regime lacking both rules and order. China may stress the rule of law, but this is only for everyday civil and criminal cases – when it comes to ideology and in particular online opinion, it no longer applies. There has never been any legislation worth mentioning on supervision of the internet – it is all administrative regulations, issued by government departments in the pursuit of their own interests. These regulations often contradict each other, leaving those who run or use internet sites damned whatever they do.

The end result is that the internet in China is no longer one unified network – it has been partitioned by supervisory firepower, just as power itself has become partitioned. Who knows how many sentries observe as you engage in debate online, who knows how many traps await. The internet, famous for its freedom, is becoming more like George Orwell's *1984* – there's a Big Brother watching all of us. Of course the internet has its nooks and crannies. Technology to reach blocked websites is developing rapidly, but it is not enough. These techniques are applied piecemeal only by savvy internet users. The majority do not have the knowledge required, and so the authorities have effectively achieved their aim – as long as only a small minority reach blocked websites they are unconcerned. A few small leaks in the dam are no real worry.

These two factors are the most important affecting the regulation of China's internet. Currently there is no force that could resolve the situation.

The only hope would be China's civil society, but this was eliminated during Mao's time, and is now only just reforming – it is weak, and no match for official power. So the authorities take the lead in running China's internet, and endow it with an increasing number of 'Chinese characteristics'. Freedom of speech, freedom of association and freedom of assembly are suffering increasingly violent attack. The internet, which should be distributed, equal, popular and free, is in China becoming a part of the system, of officialdom, under top-down control from centres of power. The face of China's internet is becoming the face of China's political system.

These trends are reflected at the annual Chinese Blogger Conference. Initially this was host to the discussion of technical issues. But the past two years – particularly 2009 – have seen more discussion of political matters and moods have become more excitable. Website administrators once concerned only with technology have become politicised and angered by obstruction and harassment. They are mostly middle class, and their thinking is, I fear, representative of their peers. The middle class should be an intermediary in society, a force for rationality and moderation, a buffer against social conflict. But if it, too, is forced towards withdrawing co-operation, towards resistance, towards extremism, then is a more worrying radicalisation of society as a whole not likely? ❐

©Xiao Shu
39(1): 47/51
DOI: 10.1177/0306422010362181
www.indexoncensorship.org

Xiao Shu is a columnist on the *Southern Weekend* in China

THE ART OF CENSORSHIP

China's strict control of online content is supported by a finely tuned infrastructure of laws and censors, as **Wen Yunchao** reveals

Day-to-day censorship in China falls into two categories. The government's propaganda authorities supervise websites that are legally licensed to carry news, while those without a license are dealt with by the public security authorities and the internet police. Unlicensed websites that are considered particularly influential may also be overseen by propaganda officials.

All news sites operate on more or less the same lines: a combination of instructions from the authorities and self-censorship. Instructions are issued requiring the deletion of specific articles. Usually, the propaganda authorities will have automated indexers that use key words to identify pages which may be of concern and, once read by the censors themselves, these pages may be flagged for deletion. The authorities may also request the publication of specific content. News sites receiving such instructions must act quickly. Instructions may range from an order to delete content, or all related content, not to publish certain content, or not to 'play up' a news item.

Website managers will establish a range of 'filter words' in accordance with these instructions, ranging from 'key words', to 'sensitive words', to 'safe words'. Generally speaking, articles containing 'key words' are deleted, those containing 'sensitive words' require reading by the censor before publication; and those containing only 'safe words' will be published immediately – although there's always a risk they may be deleted later after review.

If a forum user or blogger publishes an article containing 'key words' for that website, it will be removed immediately and not even seen for review. If it contains only 'sensitive words', it will not be posted until approved by a censor. If it contains only 'safe words' it will be published, but is still subject to review.

Successfully published articles may also fall foul of new instructions issued later. There is no unified system of key words, which means that all websites use different standards for approving or deleting content.

The propaganda authorities have established a points system to monitor the implementation of their instructions for news sites. Points are deducted if the site is found to host 'undesirable information' (even if it is not listed as such – there are numerous categories of 'undesirable information') or news from a non-approved source. In a serious case, a fine may be imposed. Points gained and lost over the year will affect the result of the website's annual review.

The Party's propaganda apparatus and the government's information offices are inevitably staffed by the same people, and the Party may opt to impose fines in the name of the information office. Sanctions on websites run by newsgathering agencies may also be imposed via the Party's own system of control – for example by instructing an agency to discipline website personnel.

The oversight exercised by the public security bureau's internet police is more straightforward – automated or manual checks identify 'undesirable content', and instructions for deletion are issued. If instructions are not followed, the case is referred to the telecommunication regulators, who will have the website shut down. The public security authorities also have jurisdiction over news websites, and often issue instructions to delete content not listed in legislation as 'undesirable' – for example, anything that shows the public security authorities or the government in a bad light.

Rules of the game

Internet censorship in China is mainly aimed at the control of news and discussion of current affairs. It relies on two supporting pieces of legislation: Measures for the Administration of Internet Information Services ('the Measures'), issued on 25 September 2000 by the State Council; and Provisions on the Administration of Internet News Information Services ('the

Internet cafe, Beijing, 1 July 2009
Credit: Jason Lee/Reuters

Provisions'), jointly issued by the Ministry of Information Industry and the State Council Information Office (SCIO) on 25 September 2005.

'The Measures' established three systems: website licensing and registration; pre-approval for certain types of website; and special approval for certain website functions. They include a list of nine types of 'undesirable information', which has come to form the basis for censorship online. Departments of the local public security authorities have responsibility for policing the internet, while administrative enforcement is carried out by bodies such as telecommunications regulators.

The authorities followed up with a range of complementary regulations. For example, on 29 December 2007, the state administration of radio, film and television and the Ministry of Information Industry jointly published Administrative Provisions on Internet Audio-Visual Programme Services. These required providers of online audio-visual services to obtain a licence from broadcasting regulators. In December 2009, a number of online video sharing sites were forced to close as they had not obtained a licence.

The most important regulations establishing pre-approval systems for online censorship are known as 'the Provisions'. These established a licensing system for websites publishing news. They include: websites run by newsgathering bodies, such as the official sites for the *People's Daily*, Xinhua, and the *Southern Weekend*; news sites established by non-newsgathering bodies – mainly internet portals such as Sina, Sohu and so on; and news sites established by newsgathering bodies to carry their own content exclusively.

The most obvious difference between these categories is the source of news – the first type is permitted to gather news, while the second is permitted only to reprint news from legally authorised sources and may not gather news directly. The SCIO has published two lists of legally authorised news sources. Carrying news from any other source would result in punishment. The requirements for obtaining a licence to carry news are extremely high and only available from the SCIO itself. By the end of 2008, there were 430,000 websites in Guangdong – just eight of which held a licence to carry news.

With this system in place, the Chinese government can use its traditional control over newsgathering to keep a grip on online news publishing. China's propaganda apparatus has a strong and longstanding hold over news production, including a licensing system, pre-publication approval and post-publication review of content, control over management and personnel decisions, and a day-to-day system of propaganda rules and notifications.

'The Provisions' list 11 types of 'undesirable information', two more than 'the Measures', and again this forms the basis for much of China's internet censorship. Enforcement of these regulations is usually undertaken by local propaganda authorities, with administrative enforcement carried out by news or telecommunications regulators at provincial level or above.

News and propaganda authorities are not just able to censor the content produced by newsgatherers – annual review of news publication licences and a points system for evaluating internal content management are also used to maintain control over websites republishing news articles. Any website which does not co-operate with content censorship is likely to lose its licence to publish news at the next annual review. ❐

©Wen Yunchao
39(1): 53/57
DOI: 10.1177/0306422010362190
www.indexoncensorship.org

Wen Yunchao is an internet observer based in China who works to remove restrictions on information and fights for freedom of speech. He was among the second group of signatories of Charter 08

Police videotape a protest outside the World Bank building, 13 April 2000
Credit: Shawn Best/Reuters

NO HIDING PLACE

Privacy is a political right and governments must not be allowed to forget it, says **Gus Hosein**

At the end of last year, the *Wall Street Journal*, in a report on the student protests in Iran, referred to a video posted on YouTube of a young woman protester chanting at the police: 'Take my picture, film my face – you can't silence me.' I hope that is the case. It is likely, however, that she will be found, and that there will be repercussions: in January, Iranian authorities warned that they were monitoring emails and text messages to find anyone encouraging protests. In the same week, Google announced that hacking attacks from China were targeting the email accounts of human rights advocates.

These cases brought to mind a recent ominous speech by Stavros Lambrinidis, a vice president of the European Parliament. He was reminding an audience of international privacy experts of life under the Greek military government. He recalled how the regime kept track of everyone's reading habits by monitoring their choice of newspaper. Through this, it was able to know a citizen's political leanings. This was a stark reminder of the chilling effect of surveillance in Europe's political history.

These stories draw the link between censorship and surveillance. A free media is considered an integral component of a new, developing or established democracy. Free speech is therefore a political right. But today we think rarely about the effects of surveillance upon an open and democratic society. Instead, we seem to only imagine political surveillance as something that existed in more primitive eras: the Red Scares; the blacklists and use of informants in the United States; the Gestapo techniques in Nazi Germany; Stalin's Russia where spying on friends and competitors and midnight raids were commonplace; FBI files on American politicians and leaders, and Watergate; East Germany's Stasi network of spies. As a result of these abuses, safeguards were established to prevent surveillance from corroding our democracies and privacy was established as a political right.

Nowadays, when we think of democratic safeguards we include fair justice systems, free and fair elections, transparent government and a free media among other components of an open society, but we rarely include privacy. Privacy is considered in occasional stories of 'Big Brother' government or as a consumer right, but we have neglected its importance for the protection of democracy. Now that society's infrastructure has dramatically changed through the expanded use of technology, the situation is even more precarious.

Privacy experts spend a lot of time speaking to sceptical audiences. Privacy is perceived as an issue of some import, but hardly on the same level of importance as other political rights. In authoritarian environments, privacy is seen as a mere convenience while the government seeks the power to do everything it can to defend the country or the state. As a result, though our talks always include a recitation of privacy's place in all the world's human rights declarations, conventions and treaties, our audiences often remain unconvinced of its importance.

In November 2008, my colleagues and I were speaking to an audience in Bangladesh on the right to privacy. We were in the last stages of an exhausting tour taking us through nine countries in Asia and eastern Africa. Everywhere we went we faced storms. Some of these were real (a typhoon hit the Philippines on our last day there) and some were financial, as the world's economies teetered on the brink. The ones that concerned us most were the political storms: some were in their early stages (we had to sneak into Government House in Bangkok as thousands of anti-government protesters organised outside), others were erupting (the opposition leader in Malaysia was arrested, again, on sodomy charges, again), and some were violent (our hotel in Pakistan was bombed a couple of weeks after our visit). Our audiences were patient, but apart from internet issues, they didn't necessarily understand the importance of privacy.

The Bangladeshi audience only began paying attention to my talk when I disclosed breaking news to them of a storm of a British nature: a Conservative member of parliament, Damian Green, had just been arrested by counter-terrorism police investigating his role in leaks to the media of sensitive government documents. Officers conducted simultaneous searches of his constituency home and office, his office in the House of Commons (without a warrant), and his London home. The leaked documents were highly embarrassing to the Labour government and included internal information on immigration issues and a list of Labour MPs considered likely to rebel against the government's anti-terrorism plans to detain terror suspects without charge. The MP's fingerprints and DNA were taken and the police went through his old love letters to his wife and his daughter's books; they also seized his files, computer and BlackBerry. They searched through his emails to discover whom he was communicating with, in particular whether he had been in contact with human rights critics of the government. Centuries of parliamentary privilege to protect MPs were swept away, as the opposition party began sweeping Green's home, offices and car for bugs. Political leaders, critics, luminaries and editors described Green's arrest as 'Stalinesque', comparing it to the actions of the Stasi or 'something that Mugabe would do'.

A police officer removes items from the constituency office of Damian
Green MP in Bethersden, Kent, after his arrest on 28 November 2008
Credit: Gareth Fuller/PA

Every time we repeat this story, and dozens of other recent examples from around the world, the lecture theatres are full of people registering disbelief. Other recent cases include:

The Bush administration intercepted a conversation of Democrat Congresswoman Jane Harman in 2005, in which she was overheard agreeing to a request from a known Israeli spy in return for support to get her appointed as chair of the House Intelligence Committee, an accusation she denies. According to former government officials, the administration did not proceed on the issue as they felt Harman was a valuable ally in its attempts to persuade the *New York Times* not to publish a news story about the National Security Agency's programme of wiretapping without warrants.

A French magazine gained access to the papers of the former head of the Renseignements Généraux (RG) police intelligence service in 2008. The diaries showed that the RG kept notes on a variety of ministers and critics of former president Jacques Chirac, including financial information, sexual orientation and habits, and histories of drug use.

In February 2008, police in the UK were accused of having contravened the 'Wilson doctrine' by twice recording conversations of Labour MP Sadiq Khan as he visited a constituent in prison. The Wilson doctrine was established in the 1960s when Harold Wilson's government pledged not to tap the phones of MPs. As Khan's conversations were only bugged, not intercepted, it was decided that the doctrine had remained intact.

These are some of the cases we know of in countries that have traditions of open government. They highlight that privacy is not a value that can be given away in exchange for security: it is a key defence of a healthy democratic system.

Safeguards are traditionally in place to protect politicians' privacy because of a belief that the ability to organise and act is integral to the political system. Collecting secret information on these individuals is a threat to that integrity. In 2009, emails were leaked in the UK which revealed that the prime minister's head of strategy and planning had planned to smear the leader of the Tory party with allegations that he suffered from a sexually transmitted disease. The plan was to allege that the evidence existed, and require the victim to come forward with alternative evidence, thereby disclosing his financial and medical records. Ironically, the British government is developing a national database of medical records from which much of this information could be accessed.

Privacy is not a privilege that belongs only to parliamentarians. The surveillance of political movements, and of individuals' political preferences, also threatens political integrity:

Colombia's intelligence agency, the department of administrative security (DAS), spied on the current president's political opponents, critics, human rights workers, journalists and members of the Supreme Court over a number of years. One human rights lawyer recounted last year that in its attempts to find evidence that he was receiving money from the guerillas, the DAS compiled a file on him which included not only financial information but also photos of his children and transcripts of phone and email conversations.

The Italian Prime Minister Silvio Berlusconi's television channel secretly filmed a judge who had ruled against him in a bribery case. In October 2009, the TV station aired footage from hidden cameras that followed the judge around, passing commentary on his actions and his choice of socks. This prompted the Italian National Association of Magistrates to file a complaint to the privacy commissioner of Italy, stating that this was an unprecedented attack on a judge, 'denigrating a person and delegitimising an essential and delicate function'.

The membership list of the far-right British National Party was leaked publicly in 2008. The list included the names of over 10,000 members, including people who belonged to mainstream political parties, police officers, soldiers, civil servants, teachers and church ministers. The employment of these individuals was placed at risk by the disclosure of the list.

Russia maintains a court-designated list of terrorist organisations. Legal experts have raised concerns regarding the vague definitions of 'terrorism' and 'extremism' in the law, which permit selective and unpredictable measures against political or media activity critical of the authorities. Human rights campaigners have claimed that the law is being used to spy on human rights groups.

Reports continue to emerge about the US government's surveillance practices targeted at political groups who pose no threat to homeland security, including pro- and anti-abortion groups, peace activists, Muslim organisations and even communities. The US has also chilled charitable giving in the Muslim community through its initiatives to clamp down on terrorist financing.

There have been a number of initiatives by the police in the UK to monitor protesters, including the use of lists, spotter cards of individuals who may 'instigate offences or disorder' and intelligence databases. The police already videotape protests and take photos of participants; with facial recognition technology this practice would be akin to demanding the ID cards of all participants.

Unlike initiatives to arrest individuals, or to censor their speech, a greater problem posed by covert surveillance is that sometimes the groups and individuals do not even know they are under surveillance. This has perhaps the most chilling effect on political organising: you never know you are under surveillance, but do not know that you aren't. When the US Congress authorised the National Security Agency's vast telecommunications spying programme, human rights groups and journalists immediately filed suit arguing that the law was unconstitutional, as it was likely that their international communications in the conduct of their work would be monitored. This, they said, interfered with their right to free speech and right to be free of unwarranted surveillance. The court ruled in August 2009 that the plaintiffs lacked standing as they could only demonstrate an abstract fear that their communications might be monitored, and that the injury is speculative, particularly as the surveillance would be done surreptitiously. In essence: you have no standing if you can't show you are under secret surveillance, and if you can't show that you've been harmed by secret surveillance, then you have no case.

All the examples I've given so far are technically similar to the schemes from days of old. The papers at the centre of the RG case in France are reminiscent of the files FBI chief J Edgar Hoover kept on politicians; the case of the membership list of the BNP is not that much different from the 1958 case when the state of Alabama compelled the National Association for the Advancement of Colored People to disclose its membership list. Modern and technologically advanced political surveillance raises the stakes significantly as it first builds the surveillance into the infrastructure of society and then democratises it in ways that Lambrinidis, of the European Parliament, observed in the practices of the Greek junta.

Modern telecommunications infrastructures are designed with backdoors to enable state surveillance. This began as an initiative of the Clinton administration when it mandated that modern telecommunications devices be designed to assist with law enforcement. The policy was then expanded in Europe, where 'lawful intercept' was standardised into protocols approved by the European Telecommunications Standards Institute. When privacy campaigners opposed these moves in the 1990s, we were admonished for not believing that democratic safeguards would prevent abuse.

Democratic safeguards and global technology do not necessarily mix well together. The technological capabilities for lawful intercept can be abused. In Greece, in 2004 and 2005, unknown third parties were able to listen to the communications of the prime minister and dozens of other high-ranking dignitaries over the Vodafone network by gaining access to the lawful intercept capabilities. To this day we are unsure who initiated the spying, which led eventually to the suicide of a Vodafone engineer. Similarly, reports regarding the Chinese attacks on Google email users indicate that the attackers targeted the company's email-interception system to gain access to communications of human rights advocates.

These same capabilities were reported to have been used by the Iranian government to monitor protesters. The *Wall Street Journal* reported that Nokia Siemens Networks, a joint venture between the Finnish mobile phone company and the German conglomerate, had sold telecommunications technology to the Iranian telecommunications company, and that this technology included the 'lawful intercept' standard (though the *WSJ* contended that this enabled data interception, Nokia states that it only gave voice intercept capability). This technology is now in place to permit the Iranian government to 'lawfully' intercept the voice communications of opponents to the government. Nokia responded just as Vodafone did: it was compelled to include these backdoors in the technology by European standards. In light of this, it is perhaps less surprising to hear that the Iranian elite military force, the Islamic Revolutionary Guards Corps, completed a deal to become the majority shareholder in the Iranian telecommunications company in October 2009.

With these technological changes, and with the advances in the use of the internet and modern databases, political surveillance no longer needs to be targeted nor does it require vast amounts of resources. Through a simple subpoena or unwarranted access, vast amounts of personal information on individuals may be accessible to government authorities, much of which would have been previously inaccessible. Recent examples include:

In October 2008, the US Department of Justice issued a subpoena to Indymedia's website administrator to disclose 'all IP traffic to and from indymedia.us'. These logs would disclose the identifying information behind all visitors to the website, all journalists and commentators who posted content. Indymedia was also gagged from disclosing the fact that it had received the subpoena.

In August 2009, Azerbaijani police questioned a number of individuals who had logged a vote using text messaging for an Armenian artist in the Eurovision song contest. Eurovision organisers later stated that they may ban countries from the competition if broadcasters disclose information about voters' identities.

In Europe, telecommunications companies are now compelled to retain the logs of customers' locations, calls, emails and other such data for up to two years. Other countries are eagerly following the European lead. In July 2009, the Iranian government announced new 'cybercrime' laws to protect the privacy of individuals that required internet companies to store all the data sent or received by their customers.

Tactics such as these are regularly used to discover the identities of journalists' sources by gaining access to telephone and email logs. Recognising
the fact that surveillance creates a hostile environment for free speech, the
Committee to Protect Journalists' 2009 study, the *10 Worst Countries to be a
Blogger*, used a methodology of eight research questions, with three focusing on surveillance.

Social networking services may exacerbate this problem. On these sites,
individuals join 'groups' or 'fan pages' and then share this information with
large networks. Sexual orientation, political interests and religious faith can
be disclosed easily. Even if this information is not willingly disclosed by the
individual, two MIT students recently discovered that they could predict an
individual's sexual orientation by examining a list of the friends on their site.
Recent changes to Facebook's privacy settings (which included membership
of groups and fan pages amongst 'publicly available information') drew the
ire of the Electronic Frontier Foundation, which noted that while Facebook
celebrates the fact that it is used by Iranians, it has now made life easier for
the Iranian government to identify supporters of the opposition. In October
2009, the investment arm of the Central Intelligence Agency put money into
a software firm that specialises in monitoring social media, trawling through
half a million web 2.0 sites a day.

Political surveillance
no longer requires vast
amounts of resources

The internet is not the sole source of additional personal information
for this purpose, however. Vast new datastores have been established in
recent years. Governments and companies now run databases that keep
information on our financial transactions, medical status and travel habits;
and they share and mine this information on a widespread basis. As surveillance again takes place often without the knowledge of the individual
under surveillance, there is no way to contest it if the government seeks
access to the medical information of critics, or telephone records of opposition members, critics or journalists. In countries where governments are
the custodians of this information in the first place, unobstructed access to

personal information is now possible. In 2008, the UK government proposed that it become the custodian of all internet traffic data, including social networking interactions; in 2009, the government pulled back a little and decided to ask telecommunications providers to monitor all internet users and to share this data with the authorities on request. Meanwhile, India copied the 2008 UK plans and recently announced its intention to collect all telephone and email traffic data for the nation.

I've always been curious why countries decide to implement censorship technologies on the internet when instead they can let individuals freely use Facebook, YouTube, access websites of controversial organisations, read articles from banned newspapers and then keep track of everything their citizens are doing. Informants and covert surveillance are no longer required when we have vast databases, telecommunications companies and internet service providers all accumulating information on our political interests, hobbies, loves, hates and fetishes.

We need to renew our safeguards for privacy as a political right. As we sell policies and products to countries around the world, we have to acknowledge the risk of abuse; and it is not some abstract risk, as surveillance appears in all political systems. My concern is that we are forgetting the political right to privacy as we are spreading our practices (from e-government to health information systems) around the world. It is thus surprising to me that audiences in developing countries find our stories about political surveillance so compelling, yet they are often ignored back home.

Throughout this article I have tried to avoid passing judgment on political surveillance. Indeed, some surveillance of political actors is useful for identifying conspiracies, illegal activities, policy contradictions and hidden interests. The task for regulating these activities is for the media and the police, with strict controls. When these methods are used politically, and without oversight, problems emerge.

We are forgetting the important role that privacy plays in our political systems, and how political surveillance is corrosive to a democracy. I can foresee two outcomes if we continue to deploy political surveillance without reflecting on the consequences. First, we may face social exclusion as people are more easily identified through their political interests. Discrimination may follow as individuals are identified as members of political groups through their donations, linked to their home addresses, their CVs and social networking profiles. The second outcome is political stagnation. At a simple level this would mean that no one would ever run for office as our private lives as toddlers, children, teenagers, and adults will always haunt our individual political aspirations. More worryingly, those in power will retain their position, enabled through surveillance of their opponents and critics.

We have long built constitutional and human rights into our political systems to prevent abuse by the executive. Free speech is one such safeguard. We cannot forget that privacy is another. This is why democracies have traditionally held secret ballots, protected anonymous petitioners, and created safeguards like the 'Wilson doctrine'. We vowed that we would not let surveillance inhibit political autonomy, development and expression. We must repeat this vow, and it must be updated and enhanced to counter modern political surveillance techniques.

The day may soon come that our whole lives and those of political activists and politicians are recorded in various databases; and someone could easily bring together a mere six megabytes of information about the most honest of us and find enough to hang you or me. ❐

©Gus Hosein
39(1): 58/68
DOI: 10.1177/0306422010362179
www.indexoncensorship.org

Gus Hosein is Privacy International's policy director. He is also a senior visiting fellow at the London School of Economics and Political Science

10th BELFAST FILM FESTIVAL

15th-30th April
www.belfastfilmfestival.org

KREMLIN.COM

Standards of journalism in Russia have not benefited from news websites. The authorities have a new channel to push the party line, says **Andrei Soldatov**

The online media in Russia is democracy's front line: it is the only part of the media that has been able to operate freely since television came under government control and the newspaper industry fell into the hands of oligarchs loyal to the Kremlin. There are a number of theories to explain this relative freedom, including the Kremlin's supposed desire to leave the arena open for the intelligentsia's discussions or as a way of monitoring public opinion. But the true reason might be simpler. The new media in Russia is unlikely to pose any threat to the authorities, dependent as it is for its content on the few surviving independent newspapers in Moscow and the regions, providing a site for disseminating and discussing the papers' news stories. Yet thanks to recent government efforts, even the online media's role as a discussion forum is now under threat.

Almost all the most prominent sites in Russia were launched in 1999–2001 by the oligarchs – Newsru.com by Vladimir Gusinsky, Grani.ru by Boris Berezovsky and Gazeta.ru by Mikhail Khodorkovsky. At the same time, the think tank the Fund for Effective Politics (FEP), headed by Gleb Pavlovsky, a pro-Kremlin spin doctor, launched a number of ambitious projects: Lenta.

Police officers detain a man during a protest against the extremism law
Moscow, 31 October 2009
Credit: Mikhail Voskresenskiy/Reuters

ru and Vesti.ru, both internet newspapers, and Strana.ru, a Russian national news service, which was presented as a new kind of media. Its websites succeeded in taking leading positions from the outset.

In the late 1990s, there were very few people who understood the internet, and not surprisingly those responsible for advising oligarchs and new media editors were often recruited from the same circle. Suddenly they found themselves in the unusual position of being asked to invent the rules and then play by them.

The first task was to define the criteria for assessing the impact of the new market. These methods of assessment remain obscure to outsiders. A new industry was born to provide the online media with the number of customers deemed appropriate for its investors: with methods ranging from pornographic banners to programming tools to increase hits. Not surprisingly, the quality of the journalism was the last thing to be considered. The top ratings were soon occupied by the news aggregators, Lenta.ru and Newsru. com. (Newsru.com was initially an NTV website, absorbed by Gazprom in 2000 during the Kremlin-orchestrated campaign that deprived the now disgraced Vladimir Gusinsky of his media empire. The website miraculously avoided the fate of other NTV projects.)

Gazeta.ru was the only website with a full-scale editorial office, with sections on politics, business, society, science and culture. It was also the only site staffed by print journalists: Gazeta.ru was created by reporters who had previously worked at *Kommersant*, the most professional daily in post-Soviet Russia.

But Gazeta.ru could never compete with the high number of news aggregators' hits and it was the most expensive website to run, given that the news aggregators did not bother to hire in-house journalists, limiting themselves to a few editors whose task was to rewrite the stories published by wire agencies and newspapers as quickly as possible. Presentation and packaging had taken over from fact-checking. At a discussion on the internet's future organised by the BBC Russian service in the autumn of 2006, both Elena Bereznitskaya-Bruni, editor of Newsru.com, and Natalia Loseva, editor of the website RIA Novosti, a state-owned wire agency, argued that speed is the most important online attribute. By then, the online media was no longer considered a threat to the Russian authorities' control of information.

The turning point was the Nord-Ost theatre hostage crisis in October 2002 and the disastrous subsequent storming of the theatre. The Kremlin found itself overwhelmed by hundreds of news messages critical of the official version of events, circulated on the internet and promoted by news aggregators. This time, the lack of in-house reporters was not an issue, for the hostage crisis took place in Moscow and some editors personally followed the events. Bereznitskaya-Bruni reported extensively on the mistakes made by the Russian secret services during the crisis and on the ensuing intimidation of journalists who covered the story. The criticism was further strengthened thanks to Newsru.com's satellite project Inopressa.ru, which translated critical stories on Russian affairs from the foreign media on a daily basis. This time, the online technologies enabling the flow of information turned against the Kremlin.

Meanwhile, the authorities had to rely on the same technology as the news aggregators, but strengthened by the vast resources of the state-owned media. As part of its strategy, FEP's projects Vesti.ru and Strana.ru were sold in 2002 to the All-Russian State Television and Radio Broadcasting Company (VGTRK), a state-owned corporation building its online media empire.

As an attempt to spin public opinion, it clearly failed. Critical stories of Russian and foreign origin kept circulating on the Russian internet, and even a direct counterattack could not help. By then the special project of Inosmi.ru had been launched to translate stories favourable to Russian policy and to compete with Inopressa.ru. The project was established by Pavlovsky's FEP and then handed over to the state-owned RIA Novosti.

Online technologies turned against the Kremlin

Over the next two years, the online media market was affected by a new development. In the mid-Noughties, more and more print journalists were losing their jobs. For many, the internet was the only area where it was possible to express their opinions. The problem was that online media had no resources to pay for investigative journalism and reportage; instead, reporters turned into columnists.

Journalists from *Ezhednevny Journal*, a weekly traditional magazine closed down in 2004, were split between Ej.ru and the newly established opinion section at Grani.ru. A similar section was created at Gazeta.ru, headed by Gleb Cherkasov, the former editor-in-chief of another weekly journal, *Politburo*, which was closed down in December 2003. Not surprisingly, the overwhelming number of columnists turned out to be highly critical of Russian domestic policy, despite lacking access to information.

In turn, the Kremlin's internet advisers had no new ideas beyond turning to the same news aggregators and communities of columnists. Meanwhile, the rules of the market had not changed: the hits still justified the means. As a result, the Kremlin recruited a new generation of experts, headed by the young internet guru Konstantin Rykov. He proposed a new and more aggressive formula for success – a combination of the same technology of news aggregators plus irreverent, patriotic columnists, lined up to attack liberals Fox News-style, strengthened by the direct and shameless buying of traffic. This was achieved through advertising on the biggest email providers: pro-Kremlin media, such as Vzglyad.ru, were advertised with eye-catching, yellow banners.

Some ends were achieved – the news websites loyal to the Kremlin were promoted to high-ratings positions, and Rykov was made a member of the State Duma. At the same time, the new patriotic media gained neither the popularity of liberal news aggregators such as Newsru.com, nor the influence that Ej.ru enjoyed with the elite and the intelligentsia.

Losing the competition, the Kremlin turned to other means already proven to be effective in dealing with newspapers: the buying of media by loyal oligarchs and the introduction of new laws controlling the press.

In 2006, Gazeta.ru, then the only news website with a fully staffed team of reporters, was sold to Alisher Usmanov, an oligarch and founder of Metalloinvest, thought to be close to the Kremlin. Early the same year, Usmanov had bought Kommersant Publishing House, and Gazeta.ru came under its control. In 2008, Usmanov further expanded his media empire: Kommersant agreed to merge Gazeta.ru into SUP Company, the owner of *LiveJournal*, the biggest blog service and virtual community in Russia. As a result, Kommersant received 50 per cent of SUP, while SUP got 100 per cent of Gazeta.ru.

This was also a time of direct state intervention. In 2007, Vladimir Putin, then the Russian president, signed a package of amendments expanding the definition of extremism. It was the second set of amendments focusing on extremism to be adopted in Russia since mid-2006. In July that year, Putin signed amendments that broadened the definition of extremism to include media criticism of state officials. According to the law introduced in 2007,

Blogger Savya Terentyev (right) speaks at a news conference, Moscow, 14 July 2008
Credit: RIA Novosti

amendments to the 'law on fighting extremist activity' require news media to label as 'extremist' any organisation that the government has banned as such. Another amendment expanded the definition of extremist activity to include 'public justification of terrorism or other terrorist activity'. It did not, however, define the term 'justification'. Other amendments regulate the production and distribution of 'extremist' material, without specifying what constitutes such material, and introduce new penalties for journalists, media outlets and printers found guilty of the offence. Penalties range from fines and confiscation of production equipment, to the suspension of media outlets for up to 90 days.

Bloggers were among the victims of the new law over the next two years. In March 2009, Dmitry Soloviev, leader of the youth opposition group Oborona in the Kemerovo region, faced criminal charges for criticising the FSB in his *LiveJournal* blog. According to experts invited by the prosecution, the information posted by Soloviev 'incites hatred, hostility and degrades a social group of people – the police and the FSB'. The charges were dropped in January.

Savva Terentyev, a 22-year-old blogger from the Komi Republic, faced similar charges of inciting hatred after posting a comment on a blog run by local journalist Boris Suranov in March 2008, criticising the police. In July 2009, he was found guilty and received a suspended sentence of one year. In October 2009, Dmitry Kirilin, a resident of Samara, was found guilty of publishing extremist statements on the internet calling for the overthrow of the regime. He was given a one-year suspended jail sentence. Kirilin had posted the comment on his blog stating that the current system of government was causing the degradation, demoralisation and dying out of the Russian people.

At the same time, the Kremlin kept trying to find new methods for dealing with the blogging community. In May 2009, the 'Kremlin school of bloggers' was launched, headed by spin doctor Alexei Chadayev, an associate of Pavlovsky. The school reportedly consisted of 80 people from all over Russia (each working with two or three activists), and their graduates are supposed to organise information campaigns online.

The biggest industrial catastrophe of 2009 was a striking illustration of the new government strategy. On 17 August, Sayano-Shushenskaya hydroelectric station, the largest in Russia, suffered an accident that caused flooding of the engine and turbine rooms and a transformer explosion; 74 people were killed. On 20 August, local journalist Mikhail Afanasyev, editor of the online journal *Novy Focus*, was charged with slander for distributing 'intentionally false reports' about the disaster. Afanasyev had been charged less than 24 hours after a journalist suggested on his site that officials were shifting their efforts away from the search for survivors too quickly. Two weeks later, a journalist from Interfax wire agency was expelled from the area of the Sayano-Shushenskaya station for his critical reporting. Instead, the popular blogger Rustem Adagamov, aka 'drugoi', who heads the multimedia department of SUP (the company which owns *LiveJournal*), was invited to report on the relief operation. So he did, reporting favourably for the authorities. In October, Adagamov was invited to join the Kremlin press pool, a proposal that he accepted.

Having got wind of the new trends, the online media started to drop their forums, fearing that a stupid comment or deliberate provocation made by a graduate of the Kremlin bloggers' school might cause the closure of a website because of charges of extremism. Ej.ru is one of the casualties: its website had become the most representative columnists' community on the Russian internet, publishing columns by opposition leaders, independent experts and journalists and prominent pro-government pundits. 'When the amendments were approved, we shut our forum so that our stories could be discussed on more neutral territory,' said Olga Pashkova, a director of Ej.ru. Other online media (including my own site Agentura.ru) began moderating their forums more closely. Vladimir Korsunsky, editor of Grani.ru, confirmed the trend: 'For sure we don't aim to close down our forum because it's important to have an area for discussion, but we will change the technology [for publishing comments].'

Today, the Russian online media looks vulnerable not only because of government pressure, but because of a lack of resources to sustain original journalism. The most popular online media do not have in-house journalists; instead they continue to reproduce stories from wire agencies and print media. For a while, newspapers tolerated news aggregators because they were considered useful in attracting subscribers (*Novaya Gazeta* and *Versiya*, for example, had even asked Newsru.com to run their stories). But what if newspapers and wire agencies, most of which have extensively invested in websites, decide to turn against the online media?

In April 2008, the news agency Interfax, the VGTRK, Gazeta.ru, RIA Novosti and Kommersant Publishing House united to protect their authors' rights. In a joint statement, they agreed that emphasis should be put on the internet, and in 2008–9 a package of means would be developed, including 'legislative and technological instruments for monitoring breach of rights'. So far, there are no signs of these instruments, but the prominent online media got the signal. Inopressa.ru stopped publishing the full texts of translated stories, and Newsru.com has recently launched a new project called Zagolovki.ru where only citations from the stories published in Russian print media are reproduced.

The new media is making a limited attempt to counter these trends. At the time of greatest crisis in 2008, more journalists were fired by newspapers, and two new internet projects were launched by former print editors: Dailyonline.ru by Raf Shakirov (former editor-in-chief of *Kommersant, Izvestia* and *New Times*) and Slon.ru by Leonid Bershidsky (*Vedomosti*). But that did not bring true journalism to the internet – both projects were business media determined to keep a safe distance from politics, and Dailyonline.ru folded in January. The oppositional political projects remain in a minority, possibly the best guarantee for survival. 'To be frank, during the years there was no serious pressure on us, it might be because we were so few and our influence on society so small that it was decided not to touch us for a while,' said Vladimir Korsunsky, editor of Grani.ru, whose office was searched in September 2003 by investigators from the prosecutor general's office.

Russia's online media continues to be essentially a new technology – not a new journalism – at best a means of distributing news already published in blogs or traditional media. ❐

© Andrei Soldatov
39(1): 70/78
DOI: 10.1177/0306422010362015
www.indexoncensorship.org

Andrei Soldatov is editor of Agentura.ru website. He worked for *Novaya Gazeta* from January 2006 to November 2008. Soldatov's book with co-author Irina Borogan, *The New Nobility*, about the Russian secret services, is published later this year by Public Affairs Books

CYBER WARS

Citizens, states and corporations are battling for online space. What happened to the dream of global communication? **Ron Deibert** and **Rafal Rohozinski** report

At the end of 2009, a social movement mobilised once again around an Iranian political crisis – from the streets of Iran's cities spreading through networks of support to Europe, North America and beyond. In Toronto, where the Citizen Lab internet research and development centre is located (http://www.citizenlab.org), a dynamic group of Iranian students banded together with activists across the world, raising awareness and building support. Together they have formed an identity unique to the 21st century: a cyber-enabled, planetary resistance community.

The role of technology in events such as these is often overstated and the Iranian case is no exception. The battle is about much more than the most recent social networking tool, no matter what label is assigned to this latest revolution. But it should not be underestimated either. Cyberspace is the domain through which the battle of ideas takes place today, and it is a heavily contested domain.

It is widely known that demonstrations can achieve broader support and publicity through the use of the internet and by the creative exploitation of mobile technologies such as SMS and video capture. But the Iranian authorities are taking active counter-measures aimed at controlling the spaces online for resistance and dissent. These measures include the well-known technique of filtering access to websites at key internet chokepoints. But there are also more offensive operations that are subtle, flexible and insidious. These include tampering with internet connections, mobile and other telecommunications services; monitoring social networking sites to identify key organisers, who are then subjected to threats and intimidation; pressurising services in Iran to remove 'offensive' posts or blogs; and arresting prominent writers and dissidents.

As two of the principal investigators of the OpenNet Initiative (http://opennet.net), a project whose aim is to monitor internet filtering and surveillance worldwide, these actions are increasingly familiar to us. What is happening now in Iran offers a clear example of 'next generation' controls that are being exercised in cyberspace as the domain becomes more heavily contested and seen as a critical vector of the exercise of power. Whereas in the past, freedom of expression activists and others concerned about human rights had to worry mostly about how to bypass internet filters, they now have to worry about a much broader suite of restraints, risks and liabilities. Rather than first generation controls, as exemplified by China's great firewall, in which filtering technologies are employed in a constant manner at key internet chokepoints, we are seeing instead the emergence of methods designed to go beyond denial to shape and contain the space for expression online. Since these controls tend to operate in the shadows, they are more difficult to monitor and thus present a challenge to rights organisations and monitoring groups like the OpenNet Initiative (ONI). They will require a new approach to research and advocacy in order to prevent the further encroachment of human rights online.

Burma 2007. Russia-Georgia 2008. China-Tibet 2008. Iran 2009. Xinjiang 2009. These recent events, although dissimilar in many ways, share several common threads. The struggles on the ground were accompanied and very much influenced by a related struggle in cyberspace, between activists on the one hand and entrenched authorities on the other. Not that long ago it would have been safe to assume the entrenched authorities were at a disadvantage, too inept to withstand digitally-enabled social movements. Today, that is no longer a safe assumption. The centre of gravity of techniques aimed at managing cyberspace has shifted from heavy-handed and often crudely implemented filtering to more sophisticated multi-pronged methods that seek to normalise control and the exercise of power in cyberspace. There are numerous examples of these next generation controls from widely different regional contexts, suggesting the emergence of a very troubling global norm. Countering all of them will require a new comprehensive approach.

Legal measures

One of the fastest growing and effective next generation controls concerns the broad use of slander, libel and other laws to restrict permissible communications and to create a climate of fear, intimidation and ultimately self-censorship. In part, this reflects a natural maturation process as authorities seek to reign in cyberspace and bring it under regulatory oversight. But more nefariously, it also reflects a tactic of strangulation, whereby threats of legal action can do more to prevent strategically threatening information from seeing the light of day than do more passive controls implemented in a defensive manner. Although new laws are being drafted to deal with cyberspace security and regulation, sometimes old, obscure, or rarely enforced regulations are pointed to *ex post facto* to justify acts of internet censorship.

Ironically, we experienced this very type of control ourselves while at the Internet Governance Forum (IGF) meeting last November in Sharm El Sheikh, Egypt, when UN officials asked us to remove a banner for the ONI's new book on the topic of next generation controls, *Access Controlled*. While the UN officials told us in person that the banner had to be removed because of references to China, they later justified the act publicly in reference to regulations prohibiting advertisements and banners in the halls of the IGF – regulations that seemed to many observers to be very unevenly enforced throughout the event (http://opennet.net/faq-what-happened-internet-governance-forum). Although examples of similar measures can be seen in almost all countries of the world, the most compelling cases are found in the countries of the former Soviet Union. In Kazakhstan, for example, opposition websites or websites carrying material critical of the government are regularly deregistered from the national domain using a variety of vague laws and regulations as justification. In years to come, we expect to see more use of legal levers such as these as a means to smother freedom of expression.

Informal requests

While legal measures create the regulatory context for denial, informal requests and other pressures made by authorities to private companies can be employed for more immediate ends. Most often these informal requests come in the form of pressure on internet service providers and online service providers to 'take down' or remove offensive posts or information that threatens 'national security' or 'cultural sensitivities'. Google's recent decision to reconsider its service

ACCESS CONTROLLED

The Shaping of Power, Rights and Rule in Cyberspace

http://www.|

edited by

Ronald Deibert
John Palfrey
Rafal Rohozinski
Jonathan Zittrain

contact@opennet.net
http://opennet.net

Internet censorship and surveillance are increasing in democratic countries as well as in authoritarian states. The first generation of controls, typified by China's "Great Firewall," are being replaced by more sophisticated techniques that go beyond mere denial of information and aim to normalize (or even legalize) a climate of control. These next generation techniques include strategically timed distributed denial-of-service (DDoS) attacks, targeted malware, surveillance at key points of the Internet's infrastructure, take-down notices, and stringent terms of usage policies. Their aim is to shape and limit the national information environment. *Access Controlled* reports on these new trends in information control and their implications for the global Internet commons.

Access Controlled is a publication of the OpenNet Initiative (ONI), a collaboration of the Citizen Lab at the University of Toronto's Munk Centre for International Studies, Harvard's Berkman Center for Internet and Society, and the SecDev Group. Support for *Access Controlled* was provided by the The Office of the OSCE Representative on Freedom of the Media.

Chapter authors: Ronald Deibert, Colin Maclay, John Palfrey, Hal Roberts, Rafal Rohozinski, Nart Villeneuve, Ethan Zuckerman offerings in China reflects, in part, that company's frustration with having to deal with such informal take-down requests from Chinese authorities on a regular basis. Such informal requests can go further, putting pressure on the companies that run the infrastructure to render services inoperative in order to prevent their exploitation by opposition groups or activists.

In Iran, for example, the internet and other telecommunications services have slowed down during public demonstrations and in some instances have been entirely inaccessible for long periods of time or in certain regions. While there is no official acknowledgement, it is noteworthy that the Iranian Revolutionary Guard owns the main ISP in Iran – the Telecommunication Company of Iran (TCI). Some reports indicate that officials from the Revolutionary Guard have pressured TCI to tamper with internet connections during the recent crises. In countries where the lines between public and private authorities are often blurred, and/or organised crime and authority mingle in the dark underworlds, such informal requests and pressures can be particularly effective, opaque and nearly impossible to bring to public account.

Outsourcing and downloading

It is important to emphasise that cyberspace is owned and operated primarily by private companies. The decisions taken by those companies on content controls can be as important as those taken by governments. Often, private companies are compelled in some manner to do the job of censorship and surveillance in order to operate in a particular jurisdiction, as evidenced most prominently by the collusion of western search engines, such as Google (up until January 2010), Microsoft and Yahoo, in China's internet censorship practices. In its most extreme forms, the outsourcing of these controls can take the form of illegal acts or acts that are contrary to publicly stated operating procedures and privacy protections. This was dramatically illustrated in the case of Tom-Skype, in which the Chinese partner of Skype put in place a covert surveillance system to track and monitor pro-democracy activists who were using the chat function as a form of outreach. The system was only discovered because of faulty security on the servers operated by Tom Online.

Presumably, many other such collusive acts of censorship and surveillance exist that are undiscovered. For governments in both the developed and developing worlds, offloading such controls to private companies allows them to place their controls on the 'frontlines' of the networks and draw in the actors who manage the key access points and hosting platforms. If trends continue, we can expect more censorship and surveillance responsibilities to be exercised by private companies, carrier hotels, 'cloud computing'

(internet-based) networks, internet exchanges and telecommunications companies. Such a shift in the locus of controls raises serious issues of public accountability and transparency for citizens of all countries.

It is in this context that Google's dramatic announcement to end censorship of its Chinese search engine should be considered a watershed moment. Whether other companies follow Google's lead, and how China, other countries, and the international community as a whole react, are key open questions that could help determine the shape of public accountability of private actors in this domain.

Just-in-time blocking

Disabling or attacking critical information assets at key moments in time (for example during elections or public demonstrations) may be the most effective tool in terms of shaping outcomes in cyberspace. Today, computer network attacks, including the use of distributed denial of service attacks, can be easily marshalled and targeted against key sources of information, especially in the developing world where networks and infrastructure tend to be fragile and prone to disruption. The tools used to mount such attacks – called botnets – are now thriving like parasites in peer-to-peer architectures along the invisible underbelly of insecure servers, PCs, and social networking platforms. Botnets can be activated by anyone willing to pay a fee against any target of opportunity.

There are cruder methods of effecting just-in-time blocking as well, like shutting off power to the buildings where servers are located or tampering with domain name registration so that information is not routed properly to its destination. Such just-in-time blocking has been empirically documented by the ONI in Kyrgyzstan, Belarus and Tajikistan and reported in numerous other countries as well.

The attraction of just-in-time blocking is that information is only disabled at key intervals while kept accessible at other times, thus avoiding charges of internet censorship and allowing for plausible denials of censorship by the perpetrators. In regions where internet connectivity can be spotty, just-in-time blocking is easily reasoned away as just another technical glitch with the internet. When such attacks are contracted out to criminal organisations, determining attribution of those responsible is nearly impossible.

Computer network attacks

Just-in-time blocking can take the form of computer network attacks. But the latter can also be employed as a component of military action, low intensity conflict, or attacks on critical infrastructures – in other words, for strategic

Anti-government demonstration led by monks, Rangoon, Burma, 24 September 2007
Credit: Adrees Latif/Reuters

reasons separate from censorship. For years, such attacks have been speculated upon and it was thought that interdependence among states served as a strong deterrent on their execution. In recent years, however, there have been several high-profile incidences of computer network attacks, including those on Estonia in 2007 and during the Russia-Georgia war of 2008. In each of these cases, the circumstances surrounding the attacks were murky (see 'Patriotic hacking' below), but the outcomes were not. In Estonia, key critical information resources, such as 911 systems and hospital networks, were debilitated, as were Georgia's official channels of government communication.

What is most ominous about computer network attacks is that many governments are now openly considering their use as part of standard military doctrine. President Obama's cyber security review, completed in May 2009, may have unwittingly set off a security dilemma spiral in this respect with its official acknowledgment that the United States has such capabilities at its disposal – a decision that may come back to haunt the information-dependent country when other actors follow suit.

Patriotic hacking

One of the characteristics of cyberspace is that individuals can engage in creative acts that have system-wide effects. This is no less true in cases of individuals taking action against those they consider threats to their own state's national interests. Citizens may bristle at outside interference in their country's internal affairs and can take offence at criticism directed at their own governments, however illegitimate they may appear to outsiders. Some with the technical skills take it upon themselves to attack adversarial sources of information, often leaving provocative messages and warnings in their wake. Such actions make it difficult to determine attribution behind the attacks – is it the government or the citizens acting alone? Or is it perhaps some combination of the two? Muddying the waters further, some government security services informally encourage or tacitly approve of the actions of patriotic groups.

In China, for example, the Wu Mao Dang, or 50-cent party (so named for the amount of money its members are ostensibly paid for each post made), patrol chatrooms and forums and post information favourable to the regime, while chastising its critics. In Russia, it is widely believed that security services regularly coax hacker groups to fight for the motherland in cyberspace and may 'seed' instructions for hacking attacks on prominent nationalist websites and forums. A shadowy group known as the Iranian Cyber Army took over Twitter and some key opposition websites towards the end of

2009, defacing the home pages with their own messages. Although no formal connection has been established to the Iranian authorities, the groups responsible for the attacks posted pro-regime messages on the hacked websites and services.

Targeted surveillance/social malware attacks

Accessing sensitive information about adversaries is one of the most important levers in shaping outcomes, and so it should come as no surprise that great effort has been placed into targeted espionage. The Tom-Skype example is only one of many such next generation methods now becoming common in the cyber ecosystem. Infiltration of adversarial networks through targeted 'social malware' (software designed to infiltrate an unsuspecting user's computer) and drive-by web exploits (websites infected with viruses that target insecure browsers) is exploding throughout the dark underbelly of the internet. Google's announcement in January 2010 that it had uncovered such a targeted espionage attack on its infrastructure is among the most prominent examples of this type of infiltration.

There is an arms race in cyberspace

The growth in this sector can be attributed, in part, to the unintentional practices of civil society and human rights organisations themselves. As our colleagues Nart Villeneuve and Greg Walton have shown (http://www.infowar-monitor.net/2009/10/0day-civil-society-and-cyber-security/), many civil society organisations lack simple training and resources, leaving them vulnerable to even the most basic of internet attacks. Moreover, because such organisations tend to thrive on awareness raising and advocacy through social networking and email lists, they are often unwittingly compromised as vectors of attacks even by those whose motivations are not political per se. In one particularly egregious example cited by Villeneuve and Walton, the advocacy group Reporters Without Borders unknowingly propagated a link to a malicious website posing as a Facebook petition to release the Tibetan activist Dhondup Wangchen.

As with computer network attacks, targeted espionage and social malware attacks are being developed not just by criminal groups and rogue actors, but also at the highest government levels. The US director of national intelligence, Dennis Blair, recently remarked that the United States must be 'aggressive' in the cyber domain in terms of 'both protecting our own secrets and stealing those of others' (http://www.govinfosecurity.com/p_print.php?t=a&id=1786).

Together, these next generation controls present major challenges for monitoring groups, rights organisations, and all of those who care about the future of openness and human rights online. Our own OpenNet Initiative, for example, developed an elaborate methodology primarily oriented towards technically monitoring 'first generation' filtering at key internet chokepoints using network interrogation tools within countries under investigation. While this mission is still essential and important, its methods are ill equipped to identify the range of next generation controls. To remain relevant, the ONI needs to adjust, perhaps even undertake a paradigm shift, and develop new techniques to monitor more offensive means of blocking. Next generation controls require next generation monitoring.

For rights organisations, darker clouds are looming on the horizon. The context around free expression has become much more ominous and militarised than it was in the past as the norms around next generation controls spread and mature. There is an arms race in cyberspace, with state militaries, extremists, non-state actors and other organisations engaged in increasingly aggressive interventions. Meanwhile, the private actors who control the infrastructure of cyberspace are also becoming more important players in determining the scope for free expression online. Together these present major new challenges and an entirely more hostile context that is becoming the norm. Arms control in cyberspace is now an urgent matter.

Lastly, citizens around the world need to be made aware of the threats to the openness of cyberspace that this new generation of controls presents. There is a degradation of valuable global communications occurring as ominous as the degradation of the natural environment. For generations, philosophers have long speculated about a global communications platform through which citizens could communicate, share ideas and develop common solutions to problems in an unmediated fashion. Writing in 1937, HG Wells presented the outlines of such a possibility in his essay entitled 'World Brain':

> The whole human memory can be, and probably in a short time will be, made accessible to every individual … It need not be concentrated

in any one single place. It need not be vulnerable as a human head or a human heart is vulnerable. It can be reproduced exactly and fully, in Peru, China, Iceland, Central Africa, or wherever else seems to afford an insurance against danger and interruption. It can have at once the concentration of a craniate animal and the diffused vitality of an amoeba.

No doubt Wells would shudder if he could see now that having come so close to achieving this very possibility, citizens of the world would allow it to implode in a spiral of weaponisation, militarisation and censorship. A planetary social movement is required today that mobilises us all to protect the net as a forum for free expression, access to information and open communication. ❐

©Ron Deibert and Rafal Rohozinski
39(1): 79/90
DOI: 10.1177/0306422010362176
www.indexoncensorship.org

Ron Deibert is director of the Citizen Lab at the Munk Centre for International Studies at the University of Toronto. **Rafal Rohozinski** is the CEO of SecDev.cyber and Psiphon, and a senior research adviser and chair of the advisory council of the Citizen Lab. Deibert and Rohozinski are founders and principal investigators of the OpenNet Initiative and Information Warfare Monitor projects, and are co-editors (along with John Palfrey and Jonathan Zittrain) of *Access Controlled: The Shaping of Power, Rights, and Rule in Cyberspace* (MIT Press)

GATE TO FREEDOM

The Egyptian government continues to harass bloggers, but they've become a vital source of information
even for the state media, says **Mohamed Khaled**

At the end of the 1990s, I was an ordinary internet user, dazzled by the
new technology. I still remember my visit to the first internet cafe in my
city, Tanta, in the north of Egypt. I sat down at the computer with my
friends, and we had to ask the cafe owner to show us what to do. He
typed 'Egypt' into Yahoo for us and opened several sites. Expressions of
astonishment were apparent on all our faces, as if we had seen an alien
spaceship.

I don't recall more than two days of my life passing since then without
surfing the internet – a feat that has been helped by advances in technology
that have allowed the internet to penetrate everywhere.

In 2004, I took part in a demonstration to commemorate the first anniversary of the war against Iraq. After that, I discovered the world of blogging.
Blogs opened up a new gateway for Egyptian youth to talk freely for the first
time, away from government information channels and the official censor's
scissors. Blogs in Egypt were still in their infancy. The majority were personal
blogs, with a minority connected to political events in Egypt. I was greatly
inclined towards politics, as I was sure that the internal situation in Egypt

Imad al Kabir, Cairo, 7 June 2007. Egyptian policemen were tried and convicted for torturing him in 2006
Credit: Nasser Nuri/Reuters

was undermined by poverty, unemployment, and corruption in all sectors of life after 23 years of rule by President Hosni Mubarak.

Two years later I started blogging. My purpose was to write about negative trends in Egyptian society, along with a little politics and personal writing. That Easter, an infamous event took place when a large number of youths harassed some young girls in the centre of Cairo. Some bloggers witnessed the incident and took pictures, which they published. Then other bloggers published them in turn. In my view, this incident was the start of the bloggers' confrontation with the Egyptian authorities. Government newspapers called the bloggers liars and the deputy interior minister appeared on a popular discussion programme to condemn the bloggers for 'sullying Egypt's reputation' abroad, despite the fact that the bloggers' real motive for publicising this incident was to investigate the astonishing security lapse that had led to it.

A month later, a video fell into my hands that heralded an unprecedented attack on police corruption. It was the video of Imad al Kabir, a bus driver, being savagely tortured in a police station. He was sodomised with a stick, and filmed on the mobile of the officer who was torturing him. That was a turning point in my life and the lives of many others. Everyone had heard stories of what happened to their fellow citizens inside police stations, but no one had seen it with their own eyes until I published the video.

The journalist Kamal Murad from *al Fajr* newspaper then contacted Imad al Kabir and conducted an investigation. The video was published around the world, and a wide-ranging internet campaign was launched against police corruption. Further videos appeared, and the police officer and his assistant were sentenced to a jail term of three years. It was not a long sentence, but it was a significant and unprecedented victory over the corruption of the Egyptian police.

In 2008, the '6 April Group' formed on Facebook to demand a mass civil protest in Egypt. It was a response to workers in the biggest spinning and weaving factory in the Middle East, in the town of al Mahalla al Kubra, north Egypt, who were calling for a strike in protest against deteriorating working conditions. The founders of this group were detained for a short time, and Egypt was transformed into a military barracks for fear of civil insurrection. Clashes took place between the police, the local workforce and citizens of al Mahalla al Kubra. There were a number of fatalities and hundreds were imprisoned: 49 people faced trial and 22 were given prison sentences. The rest were released.

The four-year jail sentence handed down to the blogger Kareem Amer in 2007, for insulting the president and Islam, marked a new era in the Egyptian government's treatment of bloggers and internet enthusiasts. Their movements inside and outside Egypt are monitored and they face harassment from security, especially if travelling overseas, when they face intense additional security measures at airports, including confiscation of their portable computers or camera equipment, memory sticks or CDs. All this, however, has not stopped Egyptian bloggers from increasing in numbers and popularity. The reliability of their information and the use of photos and video as evidence have been part of their success.

Egyptian bloggers are not threatened with the closure of their blogs. The government knows full well that blogs are free, and that any blogger will just start a new one. Most active bloggers have acquired the knowledge necessary to protect their messages and their private electronic material on the internet, and about how to resist the Ministry of the Interior's attempts to interfere with them.

Bloggers in Egypt now face a gloomy future. There are parliamentary elections this year and the government may deliberately falsify the will of the people, as in the past, to achieve a majority that will satisfy the ruling National Democratic Party. As presidential elections will be held next year, a majority for the National Party will guarantee that Gamal Mubarak, the son of President Mubarak, will be the sole candidate. This will fulfil the scenario of an agreed succession that has existed since Gamal Mubarak entered the political arena, out of nowhere, seven years ago. He was appointed secretary of the policy committee of the ruling party without any qualifications other than being the son of the president. The fear now is that most of the opposition voices will be detained, including bloggers who are likely to investigate any corruption in the coming elections. They will try to track down and record violations of citizens' rights by the Egyptian police, as well as fraudulent operations, particularly now that the ruling party has amended the constitution and abolished legal supervision of the elections.

In the immediate future, the internet will become the first and last source of news and information, for it is the fastest and most accurate means of communication, and free from the constraints of government censorship. In fact, all Egyptian newspapers now, even the government ones, have started to use many of the bloggers well known in Egypt, not only because they report news quickly, but also because of their trustworthiness. They support their investigations with photographic evidence, and show immense courage in confronting a corrupt regime. Freedom of expression will continue to be mankind's most precious possession, for without it he cannot demand any of his rights, even his right to life itself. Egypt's rulers cannot tolerate its people having a tongue or a pen with which to express their free will.

One final point. The officer Islam Nabih, who tortured Imad al Kabir and was sentenced to three years in prison, was released last year and has returned to work as a police officer in the south of Egypt. ❐

©Mohamed Khaled
Translated by Paul Starkey
39(1): 91/94
DOI: 10.1177/0306422010362466
www.indexoncensorship.org

Mohamed Khaled is a blogger and activist. He blogs as Demagh Mak on http://demaghmak.blogspot.com

BEWARE SELF-REGULATION

Short-sighted government and industry action is threatening online freedom of expression, says **Ian Brown**

One of the key protections for online freedom of expression has been the ability of internet service providers (ISPs) to give their users access to content from across the world. In the US, EU and many other nations, ISPs are protected from liability for transmitting web pages from remote sites to their users. As 'mere conduits', they do not need to put in place the extensive checks for defamation or copyright infringement required of publishers. Even as hosts of websites, ISPs are protected from liability for users' content so long as illegal material is taken down when notice is given. This is one reason there has been such explosive growth in the amount of content available on the web over the past decade.

More recently, however, governments have been looking to deputise ISPs so as to regulate cyberspace more firmly. In particular, they have encouraged ISPs to take action to address online copyright infringement, the online exchange of images of child abuse and the use of the internet to promote terrorism.

These actions could significantly impair individuals' freedom to communicate. While experienced internet users can usually get around blocks introduced by ISPs, most people are unfamiliar with circumvention tools such as proxies and encryption. Democratic governments are debating restrictions on a wide range of material, including discussions of euthanasia and suicide, 'extreme' pornography and the 'glorification' of terrorism.

Governments have encouraged ISPs to take these self-regulatory actions under a 'light-touch' rubric, with decisions to sanction users and websites taken administratively rather than judicially. Some ISPs have introduced contractual clauses that allow them to disconnect users once a certain number of allegations of copyright infringement have been made. The European Union has encouraged the development of industry-funded hotlines allowing the public to report child abuse images, following the example of the UK's Internet Watch Foundation – with some ISPs automatically blocking access to reported sites. The Dutch government has approved a code of conduct that encourages ISPs to remove 'undesirable' and 'harmful' material.

While these schemes are more flexible and less burdensome than statutory regulation, they commonly lack the procedural fairness and protection for fundamental rights that are encouraged by independent judicial and parliamentary scrutiny. Few schemes include any substantive protection for individuals' rights to freedom of expression, association or privacy. They are often introduced under the threat of legislation or litigation, agreed and operated behind closed doors 'in the shadow of the law' with little participation by or consideration for citizens.

Copyright enforcement

The music and film industries have spent much of the last decade terrified by the level of online copyright infringement. Their main response has been to launch a blizzard of lawsuits against file sharers, with 60,000 cases brought so far in the US alone. However, this appears to have had little impact on the level of file sharing, whilst generating a great deal of negative publicity. 'Band sues fans' is not the kind of media coverage musicians like to see.

The content industries are now trying to find easier ways to disconnect users and websites accused of infringement. Since 2007, they have been encouraging ISPs to filter their users' internet access, block access to peer-to-peer software and implement 'three strikes' schemes where users are cut off after three unverified allegations of copyright infringement (http://www.eff.org/files/filenode/effeurope/ifpi_filtering_memo.pdf). ISPs that refuse have been accused of stealing profits from musicians, and even encouraged (by U2 lead singer Bono in a *New York Times* op-ed in January) to take their lead on tracking miscreants from the Chinese government.

Business Secretary Peter Mandelson speaks at the Digital Britain Summit, 17 April 2009
Credit: Dominic Lipinski/PA Archive/Press Association Images

In the Irish case *EMI v Eircom* (2008) music labels took legal action in an attempt to require a large ISP to filter peer-to-peer file sharing. If successful, this would almost certainly have led to massive blocking of legitimate file exchanges, since ISPs are not in a position to decide whether a specific use of a copyright work is authorised. The case was dropped after Eircom agreed to modify its customer contracts to allow users to be disconnected if they ignored warnings of alleged copyright infringement.

UK ISP Virgin Media agreed in 2008 to send warning letters to customers identified by the British Phonographic Industry as illegally sharing music. However, neither party has released any data on whether this has reduced the level of copyright infringement on Virgin's network. Other British

ISPs such as Carphone Warehouse refused to take part in this 'educational' campaign.

Copyright holders have been lobbying politicians to make self-regulatory measures mandatory, with mixed success. France was the first to introduce a 'three strikes' law, with its 2009 *loi favorisant la diffusion et la protection de la création sur internet*. After receiving three allegations of infringement by a customer within 18 months, a governmental agency could require ISPs to suspend that individual's connection for two to 12 months. The first version of the law was found by the constitutional council to breach the presumption of innocence and rights to freedom of communication and expression. The law has now been revised and requires a judge to decide whether a user's access should be suspended.

The Digital Economy Bill now before the UK Parliament would allow the government to require ISPs to introduce 'technical measures' to reduce the speed of a user's connection, block access to certain sites, and suspend a connection – without any requirement for judicial oversight. However, the bill has been criticised even within the music industry as 'not … a sensible or well thought out piece of legislation' that is 'being rushed through the last months of a parliament of an unpopular government' (http://newsblog. thecmuwebsite.com/post/Pure-Mint-boss-resigns-BPI-committee-over-Digital-Economy-Bill.aspx). The Spanish government has introduced a draft law that would allow an administrative body to require ISPs to block commercial sites that are making available works that infringe copyright. But the German governing coalition recently declared: 'We will not take initiatives for legal possibilities to block internet access in cases of copyright infringements.'

At the European level, Viviane Reding – shortly to become commissioner for justice, fundamental rights and citizenship – has warned countries against disconnecting alleged file-sharers. In November 2009, she told the Spanish telecom regulatory authority that 'repression alone will certainly not solve the problem of internet piracy; it may in many ways even run counter to the rights and freedoms which are part of Europe's values since the French Revolution'.

At the same time, however, the European Commission has been secretly negotiating a new anti-counterfeiting treaty with the US, Japan and other developed nations that would mandate a three-strikes policy. The draft text is so controversial that last summer the US trade representative refused to share a written version with the commission, which reported in a leaked memo that 'these internal discussions were sensitive due to different points of view regarding the internet chapter both within the Administration, with Congress and among stakeholders (content providers on one side, supporters of internet "freedom" on the other).'

Child abuse images

The use of the internet for the distribution of images of child sexual abuse is clearly abhorrent, just as it is in the offline world. ISPs have been under strong pressure since the mid-1990s to try and block this content. The London Metropolitan Police threatened in 1996 to seize British ISPs' servers unless certain Usenet discussion groups were blocked. As well as complying with this request, ISPs set up the Internet Watch Foundation to set standards on the traceability of users and operate a telephone hotline to receive reports from individuals that had come across illegal abuse images.

The Internet Watch Foundation's own analysts decide if images are illegal under UK law. Reports are passed on to UK ISPs, who remove illegal content from their servers, and to police in other countries via the Serious Organised Crime Agency for overseas ISPs.

After heavy government pressure, most UK consumer ISPs now use a 'Cleanfeed' system developed by British Telecom to block customer access to web pages blacklisted by the IWF. Home Office minister Vernon Coaker told the House of Commons in March 2009 that 'the government are committed to achieving a target of 100 per cent blocking on all commercial networks … If that approach does not work, we are considering a number of other options, including legislation if necessary.' However, in October 2009 they decided that the 'voluntary' blocking rate of 98.6 per cent meant that legislation was not needed.

The UK's self-regulatory model has been widely imitated. Hotlines exist in Australia, Canada, Taiwan, Japan, Russia, South Africa, South Korea, the USA and across Europe – although lists of illegal content are often maintained by law enforcement rather than independent organisations. The EC has funded the International Association of Internet Hotlines since 1999 under its Safer Internet Programme.

The EC also funds the CIRCAMP law enforcement network, which has developed a blocking system for ISPs called the Child Sexual Abuse Anti-Distribution Filter. This is used by ISPs in Denmark, Finland, Italy, Malta, Norway and Sweden. Only in Germany has the government decided to re-evaluate this approach, running a 12-month trial that focuses on removing material at source rather than mandating ISP blocking.

Significant freedom of expression issues are raised by ISPs automatically blocking access to web content added to secret blacklists without any judicial decision. In the UK, users attempting to access blocked pages – including on Wikipedia and the Internet Archive – are usually told only that a page does not exist. Overseas sites are not generally notified or given an opportunity to contest a blocking decision. This falls far short of US free speech standards, where in the 1965 case *Freedman v Maryland* the US Supreme Court ruled that: 'Only a judicial determination in an adversary proceeding ensures the necessary sensitivity to freedom of expression, only a procedure requiring a judicial determination suffices to impose a valid final restraint.'

A number of countries' blacklists have been leaked, and apparently contain legal – if sometimes distasteful – content. Alleged blocking lists have been published from Australia, Denmark, Finland, Norway and Thailand. The Australian list reportedly included 'online poker portals, YouTube links, gay and straight porn sites, euthanasia pages, sites belonging to fringe religions as well as some pertaining to Christianity and the home pages of private companies and medical practitioners'. The Finnish list contained a site that criticised Finland's blocking system and listed blocked domains. According to the site maintainer, Matti Nikki, the national police have refused to remove it from the blacklist, and an administrative court has refused to hear a complaint even after a prosecutor declined to bring charges against Nikki due to lack of evidence (http://lapsiporno.info/english-2008–02–15.html).

The Belgian government has recently criticised judicial procedures for blocking sites as too burdensome. Its Federal Computer Crime Unit detects 800–1,000 websites hosting child abuse images each year, but rarely goes to court to have them blocked. The enterprise minister Vincent Van Quickenborne has proposed instead a self-regulatory protocol by which ISPs could block illegal content, including hate and racism websites and internet fraud, without a judicial decision.

The European Commission is now proposing to extend blocking systems across the EU, even as evidence mounts that they have little impact on the sharing of child abuse images. Graham Watson MEP, former chairman of the European Parliament's civil liberties committee, said in October 2009: 'Protection of children is a matter of the utmost importance, but this does not mean that the commission can propose measures that may well be entirely ineffectual but which will have long-term consequences for the right of freedom of communication in Europe.'

Counter-terrorism and 'extremist' speech

Many European states see the internet as a propaganda front in their 'war on terror', and have prohibited the 'glorification', 'apology' for or 'public

Motion Picture Association of America President Dan Glickman announces plans to sue individuals suspected of illegally distributing films over the internet, Los Angeles, 4 November 2004

Credit: Jim Ruymen/Reuters

promotion' of terrorism. It is difficult for courts, let alone law enforcement and administrative agencies, to interpret such vague language in such a contentious area whilst protecting freedom of expression.

Since 2007, Europol has co-ordinated a 'Check the Web' programme to monitor Islamist extremist websites, maintaining a list of URLs and statements made by terrorist organisations. While the initial project proposal suggested that 'numerous internet sites in a wide variety of languages must be monitored, evaluated and, if necessary, blocked or closed down', this has yet to occur. The German, Dutch, Czech and UK governments are investigating the practicalities in a research programme to 'address the prevention of terrorist content on the internet'. In its plan for the next five years, the EC has proposed that to reduce the threat from terrorism, 'Suitable technical resources must be made available and co-operation between the private and public sectors must be improved. The aim is to curtail dissemination of terrorist propaganda and practical support for terrorist operations.'

A number of member states are already discussing powers to require ISPs to block extremist sites. The French National Assembly is debating the *loi d'orientation et de programmation pour la performance de la sécurité intérieure*, which would oblige ISPs to block access to sites on a secret list maintained by the interior ministry 'without delay'. The Dutch government has approved a code of conduct that encourages ISPs to develop criteria for 'undesirable' and 'harmful' material to take down. The UK government has recently been silent on this subject, but in 2008 then-Home Secretary Jacqui Smith told BBC Radio 4: 'We need to work with internet service providers, we need to actually use some of the lessons we've learned for example about how to protect children from paedophiles and grooming on the internet to inform the way in which we use it to prevent violent extremism and to tackle terrorism as well.'

Child sexual abuse images are relatively straightforward to define. The international community has difficulty in finding a robust definition of terrorism, let alone of its glorification or promotion. Even the respected human rights lawyer Cherie Booth QC was accused of encouraging terrorism for her 2002 statement on the BBC that, 'As long as young people feel they have got no hope but to blow themselves up you are never going to make progress.'

Attempts to block access to 'extremist' material online are therefore likely to interfere significantly with the ability of internet users to discuss the situation in Afghanistan, Iraq, the Palestinian territories and elsewhere. Blocking would be of questionable proportionality given its limited impact on determined users. Reducing radicalisation is an entirely legitimate aim, but in a recent study of possible strategies Tim Stevens and Peter R. Neumann concluded that blocking was 'crude, costly and counter-productive'.

It is easy to understand the appeal to government and industry of 'self-regulatory' solutions to difficult social problems such as copyright infringement, child sex abuse images and the radicalisation of terrorists. Governments can be seen to be 'doing something' that in the short-term may appear reasonably effective, while reducing enforcement costs and scrutiny from courts and legislatures. ISPs are applauded for their 'social responsibility' while fending off potentially more burdensome regulation.

Parliamentary scrutiny is not an automatic guarantee of the quality of legislation, particularly when governments such as New Labour use legislation to 'send messages' rather than take effective and proportionate action. The judicial system is necessarily slow to react to a fast-changing technology and policy environment, with key cases often taking a decade to be ultimately decided by the European Court of Human Rights. Intergovernmental bodies such as the European Union and Council of Europe have acted more quickly in proposing new measures against file sharing, child abuse images and extremist speech than in ensuring the protection of fundamental rights in the information age.

Nevertheless, these are the best institutions we have for protecting freedom of expression and related rights against short-sighted government and industry action. The Council of Europe has belatedly recommended that blocking should only take place if it 'concerns specific and clearly identifiable content, a competent national authority has taken a decision on its illegality and the decision can be reviewed by an independent and impartial tribunal or regulatory body'. After a tremendous battle between member states and the European Parliament, the new EU Telecoms Package includes specific protection for users' rights, stating:

> Measures taken by Member States regarding end-users access to, or use of, services and applications through electronic communications networks shall respect the fundamental rights and freedoms of natural persons … these measures … may only be imposed if they are appropriate, proportionate and necessary within a democratic society, and their implementation shall be subject to adequate procedural safeguards … including effective judicial protection and due process.

It is now up to those who care about human rights to make sure these fundamental protections are enforced. Legislators, judges and citizens can all play a role in ensuring the internet supports the 'chaos and cacophony' of democracy. The alternative would be to allow online freedom of expression to slip quietly down a self-regulatory memory hole. ❐

©Ian Brown
Thanks to Joe McNamee and Chris Marsden for background discussions on internet self-regulation.
39(1): 98/106
DOI: 10.1177/0306422010362193
www.indexoncensorship.org

Ian Brown is a senior research fellow at the Oxford Internet Institute (part of the University of Oxford). Since 1998 he has variously been a trustee of Privacy International, the Open Rights Group and FIPR and has advised Greenpeace and the US Department of Homeland Security

Antony Beevor Historian **Professor Richard Dawkins FRS** University of Oxford **Stephen Fry** Broadcaster and Author **David Aaronovitch** Columnist, *The Times* and Author **Professor Jim Al-Khalili OBE** University of Surrey **Martin Amis** Novelist **Rosie Boycott** Former Editor, *The Independent* and *Independent on Sunday* **Yasmin Alibhai-Brown** Journalist and Columnist **Willem Betz** Emeritus Professor, Vrije Universiteit Brussel and Chair, SKEPP **Wendy Barnaby** Editor, *People and Society* **Professor Susan Blackmore** University of Plymouth **Professor Colin Blakemore FRS** University of Oxford **Geoffrey Carr** Science Editor, *The Economist* **Sir Tom Blundell FRS** University of Cambridge **Marcus Brigstocke** Writer and Performer **John Kampfner** Index on Censorship **Lisa Appignanesi** EnglishPEN **Padraig Reidy** Index on Censorship **Jonathan Heawood** EnglishPEN **Dr Philip Campbell** Editor-in-Chief, *Nature* **Sir Iain Chalmers** Editor, The James Lind Library **Jo Brand** Performer **Professor David Colquhoun FRS** University College London **Nick Cohen** Columnist, *The Observer* **Professor Jocelyn Bell Burnell FRS** University of Oxford and President, The Institute of Physics **Derren Brown** Psychological Illusionist **Professor David Cope** **Clive Cookson** Science Editor, *Financial Times* **Professor Brian Cox** University of Manchester **Alain de Botton** Author **Tracey Brown** Sense About Science **Dr Tim Crayford** **Nick Davies** Journalist and Author **Carol Ann Duffy** Poet Laureate **Kendrick Frazier** Editor, *Skeptical Inquirer* **Professor Edzard Ernst** Peninsula Medical School **James Gleick** Science Writer and Journalist **Dr Ron Fraser** Chief Executive, Society for General Microbiology **Peter Florence** Director of The Guardian Hay Festival **Ricky Gervais** Writer and Performer **Jonathan Ross** Television Presenter **Harry Hill** Performer **Anthony Grayling** Philosopher and Author **Professor Christopher C French** Editor, *The Skeptic Magazine* **Carlos Frenk** Ogden Professor of Fundamental Physics, Durham University **The Irish Science and Technology Journalists' Association** **Mark Henderson** Science Editor, *The Times* **Dave Gorman** Writer and Performer **Professor David Gordon** President, Association of Medical Schools in Europe **Roger Highfield** Editor, *New Scientist* **Sir Tim Hunt FRS** Nobel Laureate and Cancer Research UK **Sir Roland Jackson** Chief Executive, The British Science Association **Dr Richard Horton FRS** Editor, *The Lancet* **Professor Steve Jones** University College London **Robin Ince** Performer **Professor Sir David King FRS** Oxford University **Alok Jha** *The Guardian* **Dr Chris Kirk** Chief Executive, The Biochemical Society **Dara O'Briain** Performer **Professor Sir Peter Lachmann FRS** University of Cambridge, Founder President, Academy of Medical Sciences **Libby Purves** Broadcaster and Author **Dr Richard Vranch** Performer and Ex-physicist **Barry Karr** *Skeptical Inquirer* **Professor Armand Leroi** Imperial College London **Penn & Teller** Illusionists, Jugglers, Libertarians **Jennifer Lardge** Voice of Young Science network **Dr Robin Lovell-Badge FRS** MRC National Institute for Medical Research **Sam Lister** Health Editor, *The Times* **Tim Minchin** Performer **Professor Dame Bridget Ogilvie FRS** Former Director, Wellcome Trust **David Starkey** Historian **Professor Clive Orchard** University of Bristol and President, The Physiological Society **Brenda Maddox** Journalist and

Biographer **Lord Rees of Ludlow** Professor of Cosmology and Astrophysics, University of Cambridge **Sandi Toksvig** Broadcaster and Author **Dame Nancy Rothwell FRS** MRC Research Professor and President, Biosciences Federation **Dr Ben Goldacre** Writer and Broadcaster **Diana Garnham** The Science Council **Dr Margaret McCartney** Columnist, *Financial Times* and GP **Wallace Sampson** Clinical Professor of Medicine, Stanford University **Professor Alan Sokal** New York University and University College London **John Stevens** President **The Institute of Biomedical Science** **Monica Ali** Writer **Professor Ian Stewart FRS** Mathematician and Science Writer **Julian Baggini** Journalist and Writer **Professor Raymond Tallis** University of Manchester **Dr Philip Plait** President, James Randi Educational Foundation **David Bodanis** Author **Lord Taverne** Sense About Science **Baroness Kennedy QC** Barrister **Dr Matthew Cockerill** Managing Director, BioMed Central **Sir Mark Walport** Director, The Wellcome Trust **Harriet Ball** Voice of Young Science network **Professor Michael Baum** University College London **Dr John Haigh** University of Sussex **Nigel Hawkes** Straight Statistics and Former Health Editor, *The Times* **Professor Martin Humphries** University of Manchester and Chair, The Biochemical Society **Dr Karl Kruszelnicki** Author, Broadcaster and Scientist **Dr Stephen Keevil** King's College London **Duncan Campbell** Journalist and Author **Professor Beda Stadler** University of Bern **Les Rose** Clinical Science Consultant **Professor Robin A Weiss FRS** University College London and President, The Society for General Microbiology **Robin McKie** Science Editor, *The Observer* **Robin Wilson** Professor of Pure Mathematics, Open University **Dr Petra Boynton** University College London **Igor Aleksander** Imperial College London **Dr Matin Durrani** Editor, *Physics World* **Professor Richard Wiseman** University of Hertfordshire, Author **Vivienne Parry** Science Writer and Broadcaster **Professor Trisha Greenhalgh** University College London **John Rennie** Former Editor-in-Chief, *Scientific American* **Hari Kunzru** Writer **Sir Richard Roberts** Biochemist and Nobel Laureate **James Randi** CEO, James Randi Educational Foundation **Andy Lewis** www.quackometer.net **Sid Rodrigues** Chairman, Sceptics in the Pub **David Allen Green** Solicitor **George Monbiot** Journalist **Andrew Mueller** Journalist and Author **Professor Sven Ove Hansson** Royal Institute of Technology, Stockholm **Ariane Sherine** Comedy Writer and Journalist **Nick Ross** Journalist and Broadcaster **Herbert Huppert FRS** University of Cambridge **Rebecca Smith** Medical Editor, *The Daily Telegraph* **Professor Ole H Petersen CBE** University of Liverpool **Ian Sample** Science Correspondent, *The Guardian* **Professor Jean Bricmont** Association Française pour l'Information Scientifique **Martin Gardner** Author **Kristoffer R Haug** University of Oslo **Andrew Sugden** Deputy Editor, *Science* **Sir Tom Stoppard** Writer **Mike Swain** Science Correspondent, *The Daily Mirror* **David Hare** Writer **Margaret Wertheim** Science Writer **Steven Novella** Yale University School of Medicine, Editor of Science-Based Medicine and Author **Michael Shermer** Publisher, *Skeptic* Magazine and Columnist, *Scientific American* **Richard Fortey** University of Oxford **Ian McEwan** Novelist **Simon Singh** Science Writer

KEEP LIBEL LAWS OUT OF SCIENCE

senseaboutscience.org

All those listed have signed as individuals unless otherwise indicated on the statement.

The English law of libel is a threat to scientists and writers worldwide.

The recent case brought by the British Chiropractic Association against the science writer Simon Singh highlights the prohibitive costs and the limited opportunity for people accused of libel to defend themselves.

Disputes about evidence should take place in peer reviewed journals, public forums and the mainstream media, not the libel courts.

Please support the campaign to take the libel laws out of scientific debates. Add your name to those listed here by signing the statement at

www.senseaboutscience.org/freedebate

For more information contact Sile Lane • freedebate@senseaboutscience.org • +44 (0)20 7478 4380

Supported by *Index on Censorship*

OUT OF SIGHT, OUT OF MIND

Blocking websites that show images of child abuse does not solve the problem: it's a smokescreen for political failure, says **Joe McNamee**

The European Union's new approach to tackling online child abuse is counterproductive, dangerous and could ultimately lead to gross abuses against the most vulnerable in society. Over the past decade, several EU member states have introduced web blocking to address the problem of child pornography sites hosted outside the region. However, blocking merely offers an illusion of action, while pressure for effective policies is reduced and the international community fails to tackle the issue head on. As a result, citizens are led to believe that something is being done, politicians can take refuge in a populist policy and child protection organisations can chalk up an apparent success that may help ensure their funding for another year.

If there were websites which contained evidence of murder, it would be ludicrous to suggest that they be blocked rather than action taken to identify the victims and prosecute the murderers. How did we end up in a situation where that is exactly what happens with websites portraying unimaginable crimes against children? Louis Vuitton handbags and Cartier watches are given a higher priority in international legal co-operation than abused young people. Every international trade agreement signed by the European Union includes strict requirements on protection of intellectual property, but none contains elements to encourage the removal of child abuse websites. For example, the EU/South Korea trade agreement, concluded in October 2009, includes provisions on the liability of Internet service providers for illegal content. Yet the deal only covers intellectual property infringements. (The equivalent EU legislation, the E-Commerce Directive, does, however, cover every form of illegal content. Child abuse websites hosted within the EU are generally removed quickly once identified.)

In March 2009, the European Commission proposed EU-wide web blocking (the legislative process will start in 2010) and informed the civil liberties committee of the European Parliament that the measure was necessary as it is 'too difficult' to persuade other countries to delete illegal child abuse websites. Yet the United States does not appear to share Europe's worries about the difficulties of having foreign websites taken offline. In the ongoing negotiations for the anti-counterfeiting trade agreement (ACTA), the US proposed a system of 'notice and takedown' for illegal websites hosted in its trading partners' territories. Once again, however, this would only cover websites infringing intellectual property.

When it comes to tackling child abuse sites, the US's record is poor. Three-quarters of known child abuse sites are in the United States, yet the government lacks both the political will and the necessary policing resources. This shocking failure to take action cannot be explained by the legal protection of free speech in the country or by the division of power between federal and state legislatures, as some observers may claim: the worst of the websites in question are evidence of serious and violent crimes, and inaction leaves the criminals free and the victims unprotected.

For years, reports of illegal sites were passed to law enforcement authorities who were trusted to take any action necessary. Companies that hosted the illegal material were never contacted directly by either the European hotlines that receive complaints about illegal websites from citizens or European law enforcement authorities, for fear of disrupting any ongoing police investigations. The Internet Watch Foundation (IWF) in the UK has now decided to contact hosting providers abroad directly to ask for material to be taken offline (https://publicaffairs.linx.net/news/?p=1241). This change of policy suggests that the possibility of there being an ongoing investigation is so low that disrupting investigations is no longer a concern.

Treaties are cheap

Despite the lack of effective action, on average there is a new international treaty every two years banning child abuse, with smiling politicians posing

Canadian Justice Minister Rob Nicholson announces legislation that would require internet service providers to report child pornography to police, 24 November 2009

Credit: Fred Chartrand/The Canadian Press/PA

for press photos and demonstrating their determination by signing and sometimes even ratifying the agreements. Indeed, the most apparently successful UN treaty is the 1989 Convention on the Rights of the Child – every country in the world has ratified it or the 2000 Optional Protocol to the convention. In November 2009, Somalia announced its decision to ratify the convention, leaving the US as the only UN member state not to have done so. However, the US ratified the Optional Protocol in 2002.

Numerous countries have also signed the 2001 Council of Europe Convention on Cybercrime, the 1999 International Labour Organisation's Convention on the Worst Forms of Child Labour and the 2007 Council of Europe Convention on the Protection of Children against Sexual Exploitation and Sexual Abuse. The list goes on, as does the lamentable lack of implementation.

In 2007, the United States respected its obligation under the Optional Protocol on child pornography to submit a five-year report to the UN on measures it had taken in line with that 'binding' international legal instrument (http://www.state.gov/g/drl/rls/84467.htm). However, the report does not even mention the problem of child abuse websites. Given the absence of an enforcement mechanism for such treaties, the only option available to the UN was to question the US authorities. But they failed to extract any useful information (http://www2.ohchr.org/english/bodies/crc/docs/AdvanceVersions/ CRC.C.OPSC.USA.Q.1.pdf). The 'binding' obligation on states party to the child rights convention (to take all bilateral and multilateral actions to prevent the 'exploitative use of children in pornographic performances and materials') appears to be the victim of global amnesia.

The policy of supporting Internet blocking, at either a national or international level, supports this inaction. Blocking is a smokescreen for failure, postponing the day that governments will feel obliged to work on child protection with the same energy as the protection of intellectual property.

What is blocking suppose to achieve?

Online child abuse is so abhorrent that blocking may appear to be the right thing to do instinctively. As a result, the rationale behind the policy is rarely questioned, to the detriment of effective policy making. The following are the most popular justifications given.

To stop deliberate access

The Internet is designed to be resilient and to work around blocks of any kind. It is exceptionally easy to evade any blocking system that is not imposed on a global level. (And if the international community were prepared to agree to global blocking, then it would be more effective to gain agreement on taking material offline.) Put very simply, web blocking can only normally be imposed on the web proxy (the machine that locates other machines on the Internet allowing the user to retrieve information) of an Internet access provider (IAP). As a result, simply using another web proxy (using a variety of very simple tools that are readily available) defeats the blocking system. Blocking therefore cannot do anything to prevent deliberate access.

To stop accidental access

When European citizens are confronted by material online which they find upsetting and that they believe is illegal, they can report it to hotlines. However, only about 10 to 25 per cent of these reports (there were about

12,000 valid reports of illegal materials in 2008 in the UK) refer to material that is actually illegal and only a fraction of such incidents could be prevented by web blocking. It is worth bearing in mind that not all illegal sites will be on a blocking list at any one time, particularly as sites now move location and web address ever more quickly. As a society, therefore, we can either attempt to address, with the technically limited tools at our disposal, the comparatively small fraction of reports that might be adequately tackled by web blocking (even though imposing blocking on the entire population to attempt to solve this problem is clearly disproportionate) or we could look at end-user filtering solutions.

End-user filtering software requires the user to install software on their own computer and then set the software to block content based on their own or their family's needs – rather than an arbitrary measure adopted by governments for the whole population. This would help everyone to avoid accessing content that is upsetting and unacceptable to them. It appears obvious, therefore, that network-level filtering is an ineffective and disproportionate tool to address accidental access.

To disrupt commercial distribution

An unknown proportion (but one which is being allocated ever greater statistical significance, albeit without any evidence) of child abuse websites are commercial. Clearly, the thought of money being made out of this activity is abhorrent, so calls for blocking are an understandable response. However, there are only a limited number of online payment methods, so it is obvious that strong action to create the perception and reality that payment is too risky would be a far more effective solution. The US already has a coalition of online payment providers offering this service, where payments to such websites are blocked and evidence is gathered about the sites and their subscribers – and the EU is attempting to set up a similar system, painfully slowly. Once the message has been communicated that you will be tracked down and prosecuted if you attempt to pay for child abuse online, the issue of commercial distribution will be a great deal less significant.

To prove that access was deliberate

The Belgian police have cited accidental access as the main reason for introducing blocking. More recently, they have started saying that if a blocking system is in place and it can be proven that a person accessed an illegal site, intent is proven. This argument is profoundly flawed. It assumes that blocking systems work well enough to guarantee that there is no possibility of accessing a site inadvertently. Yet a blocking system can be avoided through the following ways:

- Clicking on a link to an IP address rather than a domain name (most blocking systems block the domain name, as blocking the IP address results in too many innocent sites being blocked). If your ISP was blocking http://europarl.europa.eu, clicking on this address would still work: http://136.173.160.4.
- Viruses and 'web bots' hijack infected computers and route their Internet connections through foreign proxy servers, sometimes even deliberately accessing child pornography websites.
- Increasingly, people are using foreign proxy servers to access web resources only available in that country. For example, using the anonymising software from anonymizer.com in order to access video on demand only available in the US would also result in a consumer 'bypassing' any blocking technology imposed by their ISP.
- Similarly, people are using privacy tools such as 'onion routing' to access the Internet. Internet blocking technology is so limited that, in all of these cases, users may circumvent national blocking purely inadvertently.

If there is any truth in the argument that 'accidental access' is a real problem, then accessing material, even when blocking is in place, proves nothing.

The consequences for a democratic society
While the lack of international action in investigating and removing child abuse websites would be reason enough for campaigning against web blocking, this policy also has major implications for any democratic society.

As it appears counter-intuitive to oppose the blocking of child abuse websites, this policy attracts populist measures as a tactic. Once, however, it has been introduced for child abuse websites, the door is open to apply it to controlling other types of illegal, morally unacceptable or politically inconvenient content. Even before the adoption of the Internet blocking law in Germany (subsequently suspended in the second half of 2009, without ever having come into force), a gun incident last March in a German school, involving a boy who played violent video games, led to calls for the blocking of websites with 'killer' games. Similarly, there have been calls for the blocking of pro-anorexia and hate speech websites.

There have been particularly worrying moves in Australia and Italy. Last year, Italian senator Gianpiero D'Alia proposed a law blocking any website

'Killer game' Counter Strike, 2006
Credit: Action Press/Rex Features

which defended or encouraged crime, an initiative which was given further momentum following the success of a Facebook page that praised the
attack on the Italian Prime Minister Silvio Berlusconi in December. In that
same month, the Australian domain name registry gave a satirical website
just three hours to 'explain its use' of the domain name it used to satirise
the minister responsible for imposing Internet filtering. It then deleted the
domain name.

In addition to the obvious democratic concerns about censorship
in general, this trend causes two major worries. Firstly, as proven by the
Italian and German examples, legislation tends to be a knee-jerk reaction,
with more attention paid to being seen to take action rather than proportionality and feasibility. Secondly, the Italian and Australian cases show
the extent to which blocking can be used to inhibit democratic discourse

for political purposes. Finally, in a case last year that illustrates the extent to which business interests may influence the political agenda, an Italian parliamentarian, Gabriella Carlucci, slipped up when publishing a draft law in 2009 to ban online anonymity in order to fight 'paedophiles'. She inadvertently forgot to delete the real author of the draft law, the Italian Union of Audiovisual Publishers, from the 'author' field of the Word file in which the draft was published.

It may be no coincidence that mobile operators were the first to support web blocking, followed by former monopoly telecoms operators and cable operators: they have the most significant economic interest in controlling consumer access to online resources. Once blocking is in place and has started spreading to a range of different types of content, the idea of Internet access providers influencing what users can and cannot access online may appear increasingly unacceptable. The next logical step for large Internet access providers will be to commercialise their control over what consumers can see. They may play Dailymotion off against YouTube or Bing off against Google – so that the highest bidder gets the best access to consumers. Recent agreements show that access provider policing and managing Internet use is closer than it may seem. Eircom, Ireland's biggest Internet provider, has agreed with the music industry to block access to websites accused of facilitating copyright infringement and to cut off Internet access for consumers accused of downloading files illicitly.

Blocking technologies vary between those that are useless, cheap and dangerous to those that are useless, expensive and dangerous. The simplest and cheapest technology, blocking the IP address (each device connected to the Internet has a unique, numerical Internet protocol address – a web server, hosting numerous websites often has just one address), results in large numbers of innocent websites being blocked. One of the cheapest blocking technologies, and the most popular in Europe, DNS blocking, blocks the domain name (wikipedia.org, for example), but is very easy to circumvent: by using the IP address of the site instead of the domain name, by using a proxy server that is not subject to blocking or by using a privacy technology such as onion routing or anonymiser services.

Is it likely that countries that have implemented blocking will be content with technologies that are so entirely inadequate? Perhaps, particularly bearing in mind that usefulness was never a criterion to begin with. However, the UK's somewhat more expensive 'cleanfeed' system offers the next level of ambition for those who feel the need to focus on symptoms rather than causes. Cleanfeed is a hybrid that mixes the two systems mentioned above, blocking specific files after checking the type and location of all Internet traffic. While achieving as little as the two elements of its hybrid individually, it blocks far fewer legal web pages (except for mistakes, oversights and misjudgments of the organisation managing the system, as in the famous 2008 Wikipedia case when a number of UK Internet providers blocked a page of the online encyclopaedia over fears that a pictured album cover showed a possibly illegal image of a child). More importantly, it is a hugely efficient surveillance technology that may prove attractive to the UK intelligence services, which traditionally have not been shy when it comes to asking for access to personal data.

The most chilling stage in the expansion of this creeping censorship and surveillance is now taking place in the name of protecting the music and film industries, rather than abused children. The automatic inspection of each packet of data transferred to and from consumers in order to identify and block certain material is now on the agenda. Using technology called 'deep packet inspection' (DPI), this will both allow blocking of any unwelcome (and non-encrypted) content and also allow network operators better possibilities for prioritising traffic from certain (higher-paying) sources, thereby increasing their revenue.

The obligations to be placed on Internet access providers by the legislation in the UK government's *Digital Britain* report make snooping into packets of data transferred to and from individual citizens difficult to avoid. Even before the legislation has been passed, the rot has already started: Virgin Media is planning to search through users' Internet traffic for evidence of copyright infringements using deep packet inspection (http://crave.cnet.co.uk/software/0,39029471,49304424,00.htm). Until consumers start automatically encrypting all of their peer-to-peer traffic, deep packet inspection will provide more effective blocking. Of course, it is only a matter of time before automatic encryption is added to peer-to-peer services, leaving consumers to pick up the bill for a more limited and more controlled Internet and wrongdoers of all kinds as free to operate as ever.

Thankfully, the rest of the EU is a few years behind the UK, whose dishonest populism has taken us to the stage where an Internet access provider can publicly state that it will rifle though private communications. The UK spent seven years working successfully to persuade the EU to impose retention of records of every fax, email, phone call and SMS made or sent in the

27 EU member states. The growing trend of censorship has no democratic foundation. Control of access to information online now lies with Internet access providers who did not want such power in the first place. The merging of companies and services (as demonstrated by the surveillance measures planned by Virgin's Internet access service for the benefit of Virgin's media service) will give them more and more reason to abuse the control that has fallen into their hands. ❐

© European Digital Rights - Creative Commons Attribution 3.0 License
39(1): 108/117
DOI: 10.1177/0306422010362320
www.indexoncensorship.org

Joe McNamee is EU advocacy co-ordinator at European Digital Rights

Free Word Centre

Promoting literature, literacy and free expression

'The transforming power of words'

Hire Our Space
Our beautiful hall can hold 200 people for
parties and events, or 90 for lectures and conference
Our bright and modern meeting rooms can hold
up to 18 people for meetings and workshops.
To book call: 020 7324 2570

Competitive rates for Associates
To find out more check out our website:
www.freewordonline.com
60 Farringdon Road, London, EC1R 3GA

RED LINES

Comparison with the terrorism of the 1970s is being used as a pretext for online censorship in Italy, says **Manlio Cammarata**

According to Renato Schifani, president of the Italian senate, Facebook is more dangerous than the Red Brigade, the terrorist organisation responsible for causing widespread bloodshed in Italy in the 1970s and 1980s. Schifani has stated that, '[In the social network] one comes across real incitements to violence. Though the 1970s were indeed dangerous, there were none of the collective gatherings now taking place on these sites. Thus we risk further fuelling the hatred that thrives in some fringes.' Schifani is by no means alone in his opinion. Dozens of bills to impose filters and to censure the internet in one way or another have been put forward in the Italian parliament, following the lead of countries such as China, Iran and the Arab Emirates. The conviction of three Google executives for invasion of privacy has also caused international concern.

Schifani's comments came in the wake of the attack on the Italian president, Silvio Berlusconi, carried out by a mentally disturbed person in Milan in December. Immediately afterwards, numerous groups praising the attacker sprang up on Facebook. Others expressing solidarity with Berlusconi were created as well. The minister of the interior, Roberto

Maroni, seized the opportunity to announce the umpteenth bill containing repressive measures 'to make it difficult to surf on certain sites'.

A few days before the attack on Berlusconi, thousands of people had taken to the streets to protest against the premier. For the first time, the initiative had come not from political parties or labour unions, but from the internet, especially Facebook. Is freedom of the net now endangered in Italy? In all likelihood, these most recent attempts at censorship will fail just as past ones have, but the climate is far from ideal.

Last year, Freedom House ranked Italy 72nd worldwide in terms of freedom of information. Reporters Sans Frontières ranked Italy at 49th. In both cases, the country is placed far below other democratic nations.

It should be remembered that Italy is a western nation. It belongs to that group of countries where fundamental freedoms, especially the freedom of expression, are enshrined. This right is clearly sanctioned by the Italian constitution of 1947, Article 21: 'All persons have the right to freely express their ideas by word, in writing and by all other means of communication. The press may not be subjected to authorisation or censorship. Seizure is permitted only by a reasoned warrant, issued by the judicial authority, in the case of offences for which the law governing the press gives express authorisation, or in the case of violation of its provisions concerning the disclosure of the identity of those holding responsibility.'

This is what the constitution says. The daily reality is that many things are not as they should be. For example, it is not unusual for internet sites publishing unwelcome news to be censored. To cite just one recent case, in May 2008, a blogger watched as his site was closed down. He was convicted of running an 'underground press', despite the fact that his name was clearly visible on the home page. The basis of his conviction was a questionable interpretation of the 1948 press law, wholly unsuited to the internet age. According to this law, and to the law of 1963 regulating the profession of journalism, anyone in Italy who publishes a newspaper without being a journalist and anyone who puts himself forward as a journalist without being a member of the officially recognised Association of Journalists is committing a crime. Enrolment in the association is regulated and controlled by the state, with a closed system not found in any other democratic country.

In Italy, the press is generally not as respected and authoritative as it is in other countries, especially English-speaking ones. Traditionally, its role is not really that of a watchdog. Rather, it tends to act as a mouthpiece for powerful economic or political groups. Perhaps this is one reason why Italians are not avid newspaper readers. Moreover, in recent years, the printed press has suffered from the global crisis affecting the traditional publishing world and has seen a reduction in both the number of readers and the amount of advertising. Competition from the internet is strong and publishers have yet to work out how to make online information profitable and thus offset the lower revenues coming from print publications. This is happening everywhere in the world, as borne out by the row between Google News and Rupert Murdoch, who has attacked Google for including News Corp content on its site. Murdoch has threatened to remove the content as part of his attempt to get readers to pay for online news.

The ongoing attacks by the Italian prime minister and his majority against information outlets critical of the government bear obvious witness to the difficult situation in Italy. Following the assault on Berlusconi, the majority leader of the Lower House accused the Espresso-Repubblica editorial group, some television programmes and the journalist Marco Travaglio, who was referred to as a 'media terrorist', of being morally responsible for having incited the attacker to act.

Berlusconi and his government are carrying out an ongoing campaign against opposition newspapers and journalists as well as against some reporting and investigative television programmes. Berlusconi complains about being continuously 'attacked' by public television (in actual fact, that small part outside his control). He has gone so far as to call journalists who criticise him 'scoundrels'. On more than one occasion, he has spoken of the 'criminal use of television'. The 'Bulgarian edict' of 2002, when the prime minister criticised the behaviour of some journalists and TV stars during a press conference with the prime minister of Bulgaria, after which the journalists Enzo Biagi and Michele Santoro, as well as the comedian Daniele Luttazzi, lost their jobs with Rai, is still a noteworthy example of what goes on.

This kind of intimidation has been the norm for the past 15 years. It began when Berlusconi, a television entrepreneur, entered the political arena and started leading the government in the absence of effective legislation against conflicts of interest. Ever since then, political power and 'television power' have been in the hands of a lone individual. The consequences are there for all to see.

The implications for democracy are serious, as television in Italy continues to be the most powerful medium influencing public opinion. Uncontested statistics indicate that between 70 and 80 per cent of the Italian population receives information and forms its political opinions through television. Notably, around 90 per cent of Italian television is under the premier's control. Indeed, Berlusconi owns most of Italy's

private television system via three national networks. Moreover, in his role as head of government, he indirectly controls the public television system as its board members are appointed so as to represent the parliamentary majority. A member of the board, key in taking decisions, is directly appointed by the government. In 2004, the European parliament observed 'that the Italian system presents an anomaly owing to a unique combination of economic, political and media power in the hands of one man, the current president of the Italian council of ministers and to the fact that the Italian government is, directly or indirectly, in control of all national television channels'.

Berlusconi's power also extends to those publishing houses not part of his economic-political empire. In December 2008, he railed against the press, saying that 'politicians and directors of newspapers such as *La Stampa* and *Corriere della Sera* should all change professions, should all go home'. Perhaps it is just a coincidence that a new director was appointed at *Corriere* in March 2009 and at *La Stampa* in April.

Berlusconi is carrying out an ongoing campaign against opposition journalists

Italy has six leading national television channels, three of which, Rai Uno, Rai Due and Rai Tre, are public service stations. The three others, Canale 5, Italia 1 and Rete 4, are private channels. These last three are directly owned by Berlusconi via Mediaset. In effect, though, he controls five of the six channels: in addition to the three Mediaset stations, he has appointed the network directors and television news programme directors of the first two public broadcasting channels. Only the third, for historical reasons, remains in part under the control of the left-wing opposition. However, on average, its audience levels are lower than those of the first two channels, partly because it has fewer economic and organisational resources. Mention must also be made of the news programme aired by La7, a broadcaster owned by Telecom Italia, Italy's leading telecommunications company, and by the satellite channels RaiNews24 and Sky News 24. On the whole, their audiences are not large. The lion's share of viewers choose Rai's TG1 and Mediaset's TG5.

Silvio Berlusconi, from Erik Gandini's film Videocracy, *2009*
Credit: Atmo, www.atmo.se

The system is tightly controlled. In 1999, following a call for tenders from different television operators, Europa 7 won the licence to broadcast nationwide. Ten years on and it is still not on air. This is despite the latest in a long series of decisions, both by the Italian courts and the EU, recognising the channel's right to operate, as it has yet to be assigned enough frequencies sufficient to broadcast nationwide.

The scenario could change with the switch to digital terrestrial television. Today, around 30 per cent of the Italian population has digital television and thus access to a large number of channels. Rupert Murdoch's Sky Italia pay-TV satellite channel has already achieved some success but his attempt to launch Cielo, a free digital service to rival Mediaset's and Rai's supremacy, was initially blocked by the Italian government on the grounds of concerns over competition issues. It was stopped from making its debut on 1 December but, following a green light from the European Commission, it began broadcasting two weeks later. Hopes that it will provide a healthy jolt to broadcast news have been dented by scheduling. Its news programme is not aired during primetime but at 7am, 12 noon and 7pm. This way it does not compete with the news programmes controlled by Berlusconi but with the only independent one, TG3, airing at the same time. Consequently, the Italian anomaly is far from being resolved. On the contrary, it has only worsened.

Another situation illustrating how public television is constantly penalised by politics is the controversy surrounding the new satellite broadcaster Tivù Sat, the product of a joint venture between Rai and Mediaset and in which La7 has a small stake. At the start of 2009, it was put forward as a free satellite platform to serve that part of the population (around 10 per cent) unable to receive terrestrial digital television. With this aim in mind, Rai removed some of its subject-based channels from the Sky platform and began to encrypt a growing number of programmes aired by the three general channels rebroadcast from Murdoch's platform. Consequently, both Rai and Sky suffered considerable damage, while Berlusconi's company maintained its positions. And that's not all. For reasons that are not easy to understand, an encryption system not supported by decoders available on the market was selected for the new satellite programme, forcing users to acquire a new decoder not available in shops. As a result, a portion of users are unable to view many of the programmes shown on public television, for which they pay a licence fee. Fortunately, the communications authority intervened in December and declared it mandatory to broadcast public services on all technological platforms and to provide all citizens and Italians residing abroad with the card needed to see Tivù Sat channels, without forcing them to purchase a special decoder.

At the end of February, ahead of the regional elections, the parliamentary watchdog commission in charge of overseeing radio and television services effectively banned political talk shows, when it ruled that discussion programmes had to feature each political party — an unworkable demand. This is the situation in Italy at the start of 2010. It is not freedom of expression that is lacking, but citizens' freedom to receive complete and impartial information. ❐

©Manlio Cammarata
Translated by Susan Grace
39(1): 119/125
DOI: 10.1177/0306422010362147
www.indexoncensorship.org

Manlio Cammarata is a journalist and expert on law and information technology. He runs the site www.mcreporter.info

IF THEY DISAPPEAR...
WHO WILL KEEP US INFORMED?

PRENSA

AUCION

UCION

PRECAU

Photo by Luz Montero

WHAT YOU DON'T KNOW
CAN HURT YOU
Permanent Campaign to Protect Journalists in México

www.libertad-expresion.org.mx

TOOLS OF THE TRADE

As filtering becomes increasingly commonplace, **Roger Dingledine** reviews the options for beating online censorship

As more countries crack down on internet use by filtering connections to sensitive websites, people around the world are increasingly turning to anti-censorship software, also known as circumvention tools. A wide variety of tools have been built to answer this threat by letting people get to websites they otherwise can't reach. But different tools provide different features and varying levels of security, and it's hard for users to understand the trade-offs.

This article lays out ten features you should consider when evaluating a circumvention tool. The goal isn't to advocate for any specific tool, but to point out what kind of tools are useful for different situations. In fact, having a diversity of circumvention tools in wide use increases robustness for all the tools, since censors have to tackle every strategy at once.

One caveat to start out: I'm an inventor and developer of a tool called Tor (torproject.org) that is used both for privacy and for circumvention. While my bias for more secure tools like Tor is evident here, based on which features I've picked (meaning I raise issues that highlight Tor's strengths and that some other tool developers may not care about), I have also tried to include features that other tool developers consider important.

How it works

Internet-based circumvention software consists of two components: a relaying component and a discovery component. The relaying component is what establishes a connection to some server or proxy, handles encryption and sends traffic back and forth. The discovery component is the step before that – the process of finding one or more reachable addresses.

Some tools have a simple relaying component. For example, if you're using an open proxy, the process of using the proxy is straightforward: you configure your web browser or other application to use it. The big challenge for open proxy users is finding an open proxy that's reliable and fast. On the other hand, other tools have much more sophisticated relaying components, made up of multiple proxies, multiple layers of encryption and so on.

The more the merrier

One of the first questions you should ask when looking at a circumvention tool is who else uses it. A wide variety of users means that if somebody finds out you're one of the users, they can't conclude much about why you're using it, or what sort of person you are.

At one extreme, imagine a hypothetical circumvention tool given out only to a select group of Iranian bloggers. If anybody discovers that you're using it, they can guess who are you and what you're doing with it. At the other extreme, a privacy tool like Tor has many different classes of users around the world (ranging from ordinary people, civil rights enthusiasts, and human rights activists to corporations, law enforcement, and the military) so the fact that you have Tor installed doesn't give people much additional information about who you are or what sort of sites you might visit.

Beyond technical features that make a given tool useful to a narrow audience or a broader audience, marketing plays a big role in which users show up. A lot of tools spread through word of mouth, so if the first few users are in Vietnam and they find it useful, the next set of users will tend to be from Vietnam too. Whether a tool is translated into some languages but not others can also direct (or hamper) which users it will attract.

Access for all?

The next question to consider is whether the tool operator artificially restricts which countries can use it. Several years ago, the commercial Anonymizer. com made its service free to people in Iran. Thus connections coming from Anonymizer's servers were either paying customers (mostly in America) or people in Iran trying to get around their country's filters.

An internet user tries to log onto social networking site Facebook in Tehran, 25 May 2009
Credit: Morteza Nikoubazl/Reuters

مشترک گرامی

دسترسی به این سایت امکان پذیر نمی باشد

در صورتی که این سایت به اشتباه فیلتر شده است با پست الکترونیکی

filter@dci.ir

با درج نام دامنه مورد نظر در موضوع نامه و ارائه توضیحات لازم

مکاتبه فرمائید

For more recent examples, Your Freedom (your-freedom.net) restricts free usage to a few countries like Burma, while systems like Freegate (dit-inc.us) and Ultrasurf (ultrareach.com) outright block connections from all but the few countries that they care to serve (China and, in the case of Ultrasurf recently, Iran). On the one hand, this strategy makes sense in terms of limiting the bandwidth costs. But on the other hand, if you're in Saudi Arabia and need a circumvention tool, some otherwise useful tools are simply not an option for you.

Survival of the fittest

If you're going to invest the time to figure out how to use a given tool, you want to make sure it's going to be around for a while. Different tools take different approaches to ensuring their long-term existence. The main three approaches are through volunteers, through profit, and through sponsors.

Networks like Tor rely on volunteers to provide the relays that make up the network. Thousands of people around the world have computers with good network connections and want to help make the world a better place. By joining them into one big network, Tor ensures that the network is independent from the entity writing the software; so the network will survive even if the Tor Project ceases to exist.

Psiphon (psiphon.ca), by contrast, is taking the for-profit approach of collecting money for service. They reason that if they can create a profitable company, then that company will be able to fund all of their costs (including the network) on an ongoing basis. The third approach is to rely on sponsors to pay for the bandwidth costs. The Java Anon Proxy or JAP project (anon.inf.tu-dresden.de/index_en.html) relied on government grants to fund its bandwidth; now that the grant has finished they're investigating the for-profit approach. Ultrareach and Freegate use the 'sponsor' model to good effect, though they are constantly hunting for further sponsors to keep their network operational.

After considering the sustainability of the network, the next question is the software itself. The same three approaches apply here, but the examples change. While Tor's network is operated by volunteers, Tor relies on sponsors (governments and NGOs) to fund new features and software maintenance. Ultrareach and Freegate, on the other hand, are in a more sustainable position with respect to software updates: they have a team of individuals around the world, mostly volunteers, dedicated to making sure the tools are one step ahead of censors.

Each of the three approaches can work. The key when evaluating a tool is to understand which approaches that tool uses, so you can predict what problems it might encounter in the future.

Open design

The first step to transparency and reusability of the tool's software and design is to distribute the software (not just the client-side software, but also the server-side software) under an open source licence. Open source licences make sure you can examine the software to see how it really operates, and they also mean that you have the right to modify the program. Even if not every user takes advantage of this opportunity (many people just want to use the tool as it is, after all), the fact that it can be modified makes it much more likely that the tool will remain safe and useful. Without this option, you are forced to trust that a small number of developers have thought of and addressed every possible problem.

Just having an open software licence is not enough. Trustworthy circumvention tools need to provide clear complete documentation for other security experts – not just how it's built, but what features and goals its developers aimed for. Do they intend it to provide privacy? If so, what kind of privacy and against what kind of attackers? In what way does it use encryption? Do they intend it to stand up to attacks from censors? What kind of attacks do they expect to resist and why will their tool resist them? Without both seeing the source code and knowing what the developers meant for it to do, it's harder to decide whether there are security problems in the tool or to evaluate how successful it should be at its goals.

In the field of cryptography, Kerckhoffs' principle explains that you should design your system so the amount you need to keep secret is as minimal and well understood as possible. That's why crypto algorithms have keys (the secret part) and the rest can be explained in public to anybody. Historically, any crypto design that has a lot of secret parts has turned out to be less safe than its designers thought. Similarly, in the case of secret designs for circumvention tools, the only groups examining the tool are its original developers and its attackers; the wider user and developer community is left out of the loop.

This question brings us to another important concern regarding another form of sustainability: whether the ideas from a project have a use beyond its lifetime. Too many circumvention tools these days keep many parts of their design secret, in hopes that government censors are hampered from figuring out how the system works. The result is that few projects can learn from other projects and the field of circumvention development as a whole moves forward too slowly.

Privacy by design

Another feature to look for in a circumvention tool is whether its network is centralised or decentralised. A centralised tool puts all of its users' requests

Chinese police raid an illegal internet cafe in Guangzhou, 20 June 2002
Credit: China Photos/Reuters

through one or a few servers that the tool operator controls. A decentralised design like Tor or JAP sends the traffic through multiple different locations, so there is no single location or entity that is aware of which websites each user is accessing.

Another way to look at this division is based on whether the trust is centralised or decentralised. If you have to put all your trust in one entity, then the best you can hope for is 'privacy by policy' – meaning they have all your data and they promise not to look at it, lose it, sell it and so on. The alternative is 'privacy by design', a phrase popularised by the Ontario Privacy Commissioner – meaning the design of the system itself ensures that users get their privacy. The openness of the design in turn lets everybody evaluate the level of privacy provided.

This concern isn't just theoretical. In early 2009, Hal Roberts from the Berkman Center ran across a FAQ entry for a circumvention tool that offered to sell its users' clicklogs. I later talked to a different circumvention tool provider who explained that they had all the logs of every request ever made through their system 'because you never know when you might want them'.

I've left out the names of the tools here, because the point is not that some tool providers may have shared user data; the point is that any tool with a centralised trust architecture could share user data, now or in the future, and its users have no way to tell whether it's happening. Worse, even if the tool provider means well, the fact that all the data flows through a few servers creates an attractive target for other attackers to come snooping.

The next conclusion is that many of these tools see circumvention and user privacy as totally unrelated goals. This separation isn't necessarily bad, as long as you know what you're getting into. For example, we hear from many people in censoring countries that just reading a news website isn't going to get you locked up. But as we've been learning in many other contexts over the past few years, large databases of personal information tend to end up more public than we'd like.

Keeps you safe from websites too

Privacy isn't only about whether the tool operator can log your requests. It's also about whether the websites you visit can recognise or track you. Circumvention tools have some level of built-in protection here, since using a proxy means the website doesn't see the user's connection directly. But remember the case of Yahoo turning over information about one of its Chinese webmail users. What if a blog aggregator wants to find out who's posting to a blog, or who added the latest comment, or what other websites a particular blogger reads?

At one extreme are open proxies that often pass along the address of the client with their web request, so it's easy for the website to learn exactly where the request is coming from. At the other extreme are tools like Tor that include client-side browser extensions to hide your browser version, language preference, browser window size, time zone and so on; segregate cookies, history and cache; and prevent plugins like Flash from leaking information about you.

This type of application level protection comes at a cost though: some websites don't work correctly. As more websites move to the latest web 2.0 fads, they require more and more invasive features with respect to browser behaviour. The safest answer is to disable the dangerous behaviours – but if somebody in Turkey is trying to reach Youtube and Tor disables his Flash plugin to keep him safe, his videos won't work.

No tools have solved this trade-off well yet. Psiphon manually evaluates each website and programmes its central proxy to rewrite each page. Mostly they do this rewriting not for privacy, but to make sure all links on the page lead back to their proxy service. The result is that if they haven't manually vetted your destination site yet, it won't work for you. As an example, they seem to be in a constant battle to keep up with Facebook's changing front page. Tor currently disables many sites that are probably safe in practice, because we haven't figured out a good interface to let the user decide in an informed way. Other tools just let through any active content, meaning it's trivial to unmask their users.

No magic formula

I should draw a distinction here between privacy and encryption. Most circumvention tools (all but the really simple ones like open proxies) encrypt the traffic between the user and the circumvention provider. They need this encryption to avoid the keyword filtering done by censors such as China's firewall. But none of the tools can encrypt the traffic between the provider and the destination websites – if a destination website doesn't support encryption, there's no magic way to make the traffic encrypted.

The ideal answer would be for everybody to use https (also known as SSL) when accessing websites, and for all websites to support https connections. When used correctly, https provides encryption between your web browser and the website. This 'end-to-end' encryption means nobody on the network (not your ISP, not the backbone internet providers, and not your circumvention provider) can listen in on the contents of your communication. But for a wide variety of reasons, pervasive encryption hasn't taken off.

If the destination website doesn't support encryption, the best you can do is (1) not send identifying or sensitive information, such as a real name in a blog post or a password you don't want other people to learn, and then (2) use a circumvention tool that doesn't have any trust bottlenecks that allow somebody to link you to your destinations despite the precautions in step 1.

Alas, things get messy when you can't avoid sending sensitive info. Some people have expressed concern over Tor's volunteer-run network design, reasoning that at least with the centralised designs you know who runs the infrastructure. But in practice it's going to be strangers reading your traffic either way – the trade-off is between volunteer strangers who don't know it's you (meaning they can't target you) or dedicated strangers who get to see your entire traffic profile (and link you to it). Anybody who promises '100 per cent security' is selling something.

The need for speed

The next feature you might look for in a circumvention tool is speed. Some tools tend to be consistently fast, some consistently slow, and some provide wildly unpredictable performance. Speed is based on many factors, including how many users the system has, what the users are doing, how much capacity there is, and whether the load is spread evenly over the network.

The centralised-trust designs have two advantages here. First, they can see all their users and what they're doing, meaning they have a head start at spreading them out evenly and at discouraging behaviours that tax the system. Second, they can buy more capacity as needed, so the more they pay the faster the tool is. The distributed-trust designs on the other hand have a harder time tracking their users, and if they rely on volunteers to provide capacity, then getting more volunteers is a more complex process than just paying for more bandwidth.

The flip side of the performance question is flexibility. Many systems ensure good speed by limiting what their users can do. While Psiphon prevents you from reaching sites that they haven't manually vetted, Ultrareach and Freegate actually actively censor which destination websites you're allowed to reach so they can keep their bandwidth costs down. Tor, by contrast, lets you access any protocol and destination, meaning for example you can instant message through it too; but the downside is that the network is often overwhelmed by users doing bulk transfer.

Getting started

Once a circumvention tool becomes well known, its website is going to get blocked. If it's impossible to get a copy of the tool itself, who cares how good it is? The best answer here is to not require any specialised client software. Psiphon, for example, relies on a normal web browser, so it doesn't matter if the censors block their website. Another approach is a tiny program like Ultrareach or Freegate that you can instant message to your friends. Option three is Tor's Browser Bundle: it comes with all the software you need preconfigured, but since it includes large programs like Firefox, it's harder to pass around online. In that case, distribution tends to be done through social networks and USB sticks, or using our email autoresponder that lets you download Tor via Gmail.

Then you need to consider the trade-offs that come with each approach. First, which operating systems are supported? Psiphon wins here too by not requiring any extra client software. Ultrareach and Freegate are so specialised that they only work on Windows, whereas Tor and its accompanying software will build and run pretty much everywhere. Next, consider that client-side software can automatically handle failover from one proxy to the next, so you don't need to manually type in a new address if your current address disappears or gets blocked.

The final question is whether the tool has a track record, or at least a convincing plan, for responding to blocking. For example, Ultrasurf and Freegate have a history of releasing quick updates when the current version of their tool stops working. They have a lot of experience at this particular cat-and-mouse game, so it's reasonable to assume they're ready for the next round. Along these lines, Tor prepared for its eventual blocking by streamlining its network communications to look more like encrypted web browsing, and introducing unpublished 'bridge relays' that are harder for an attacker to find and block than Tor's public relays. Tor tries to separate software updates from proxy address updates – if the bridge relay you're using gets blocked, you can stick with the same software and just configure it to use a new bridge address. Our bridge design was put to the test in China last September, and tens of thousands of users seamlessly moved from the public relays to bridges.

Keeping a low profile

Many circumvention tools launch with a huge media splash. The media love this approach, and they end up with front-page articles like 'American hackers declare war on China!' But while this attention helps attract support (volunteers, profit, sponsors), the publicity also draws the attention of the censors.

Censors generally block two categories of tools: the ones that are working really well, meaning they have hundreds of thousands of users, and the ones that make a lot of noise. In many cases, censorship is less about blocking all sensitive content and more about creating an atmosphere of repression so people end up self-censoring. Articles in the press threaten the censors' appearance of control, so they are forced to respond.

The lesson here is that we can control the pace of the arms race. Even if a tool has many users, as long as nobody talks about it much it tends not to get blocked. But if nobody talks about it, how do users learn about it? One way out of the paradox is to use word of mouth and social networks rather than the more traditional media. Another approach is to position the tool in a different context – for example, we present Tor primarily as a privacy and civil liberties tool rather than a circumvention tool. Alas, this balancing act is tough to maintain in the face of increasing popularity.

Last, we should keep in mind that technology won't solve the whole problem. After all, firewalls are socially very successful in authoritarian countries. As long as many people in censored countries are saying, 'I'm so glad my government keeps me safe on the internet,' the social challenges are at least as important. But at the same time, there are people in all of these countries who want to learn and spread information online, and a strong technical solution remains a critical piece of the puzzle. ❐

©Roger Dingledine
39(1): 127/137
DOI: 10.1177/0306422010363345
www.indexoncensorship.org

Roger Dingledine is project leader for The Tor Project, a US non-profit working on anonymity research and development for such diverse organizations as the US Navy, the Electronic Frontier Foundation and Voice of America

POWER TO THE PEOPLE

The Iranian state is working hard to crush grass-roots dissent and its ability to organise itself through the internet. It will ultimately fail, says **Saeed Valadbaygi**

The explosion in the use of the internet in Iran in recent months, as part of the anti-government protests, has often been the focus of attention by foreign observers. But the internet is just one of the tools being used in this revolution of the people. The important role played by several underground newspapers and satellite television stations should not be ignored, nor the fact that this popular dissent has all taken place against the backdrop of heavy censorship, the blocking of internet sites, restrictions in the use of the latest technology and the disruption of signals for television and radio networks.

The Islamic Republic's treatment of the media, journalists and political activists mirrors all the devices of the 30-year rule of a government that has been frightened to allow its citizens freedom of expression and dreaded their being influenced by the outside world. The banning of foreign journalists, imprisonment of Iranian journalists and media activists, the closure of opposition newspapers, the raiding of citizens' homes to seize satellite dishes, the monitoring of personal telephone calls, the filtering and disruption of internet services are all part of the state's policy of intimidation.

Internet cafe, Tehran, January 2009
Credit: Fernando Moleres/Panos

Many politicians and experts both inside and outside the country believe the time has come to break the wall of censorship in Iran and set out demands. In July 2009, the US Senate voted unanimously to take action against censorship in Iran, allocating a budget of up to $55m as part of the Victims of Iranian Censorship Act (VOICE) to help Iranians evade their government's attempts to censor the internet and to put pressure on foreign companies not to help Iran in its repressive measures.

Yet in many cases computer companies have boycotted their own products, thus exacerbating the problem for Iranian users. One group founded in 2004 for the struggle against censorship in Iran says: 'We have grievances against governments who with funding for the fight against censorship have the intention of supporting freedom of information and expression, for they haven't truly supported or assisted users or campaigners. Our question is this: with the provision of such sizeable budgets why have companies like DIT Software blocked Freegate [software to allow users to view blocked sites] in Iran and only Iran in such critical circumstances? Why aren't experts within Iran – who have the capability of designing software to bypass filtering – supported? And in truth where are these budgets that are approved in the name of Iranians spent? And on whom?'[1]

The experience of Iran's citizen media is a good illustration that independent media and social networking sites can play a significant role in the advancement of grass-roots movements. If, in the past, human rights activists and political leaders suffered many obstacles in expressing their ideas and implementing action, today we see that opinion and votes lie side by side, giving people the possibility of choice and control. In the current climate, the media holds special significance for the people of Iran. Throughout Iran's history there has been controversy regarding a free press and freedom of expression that ultimately led to the establishment of a dictatorship.

Finally, what matters, and is crucial, is that an independent people's media can still perform in the same way as parties, unions and institutions, playing a pivotal role in reflecting the beliefs and desires of different groups in society, and remain a tool of threat and pressure for the masses against the government. Perhaps if the generation before us had the tools of today during the 1979 revolution, they would have made decisions based on more analysis and reasoning and prevented the human disasters of these past 30 years. A clear difference between the Iran of today and that of the past is the independent and unified media that has arisen from the tools of social interaction. ❐

1. DIT have responded that they had to limit Freegate use in Iran to a few news sites as their services were overloaded by traffic from Iran in June 2009 and caused service disruption.

©Saeed Valadbaygi
Translated by Negar Esfandiary
39(1): 138/140
DOI: 10.1177/0306422010362189
www.indexoncensorship.org

Saeed Valadbaygi, 27, is a journalist and blogger. He was imprisoned three times for his activities, and escaped from prison hospital during his third incarceration. His blogs, including Revolutionary Road, have been hacked by the Iranian government numerous times. His website astreetjournalist.com http://www.astreetjournalist.com/ received more than 15 million hits during the recent 27 December 2009 demonstrations

How Censorship Works

Institutions like the Supreme Council of the Cultural Revolution and the Supreme Information Council issue directives limiting access to Internet sites. The Islamic Republic was aware of the potential dangers of a people's media and, as seen in other dictatorships, began extensive filtering. The Internet is the main focus of government censorship. A passing glance at some of its features immediately shows why this tool of digital democracy clashes with the politics of the Islamic Republic. It is a form of media capable of reaching everyone. It is not bound by time or location, it's quick and costs little, it makes research and gathering of information easy – networks are connected to each other, users can easily participate by producing content or adding information. News and information can easily reach a source or become a subject followed by others and even become the main focus. Censorship was at first carried out on the pretext of restricting websites that were 'immoral' or 'against values', but the government's record in filtering illustrates that even before moral issues became the main focus, fear of an opposing voice and freedom of expression in political and social matters were at the root of this task.

Currently a three-member committee consisting of representatives of Sound and Vision (state media), the Ministry of Culture and the Information Ministry make decisions with respect to accessing Internet sites or the restriction of them on behalf of the Supreme Council of the Cultural Revolution. In many cases we've witnessed the blocking of sites announced directly by Iran's judiciary. Most of the victims of this censorship machine are Persian language personal blogs and news sites, also porn and other sexually orientated sites that are all filtered in Iran.

The other method used for creating disruption in accessing the Internet is the slowing down of servers. In ten years of Internet use in Iran, the speed remains unchanged. This, compared to a growth rate of a few hundred per cent in other countries worldwide, is another affirmation of efforts to restrict knowledge in Iran.

All this takes place in a land where some 800,000 Persian language blogs and thousands of alternative websites are created in the shortest time possible, sharing social and political events in film and audio – a phenomenon that does not bode well for the Islamic Republic or any dictatorship. In a population of around 70 million, Iran has more than 18 million Internet users. The Islamic Republic, in accordance with its political ideology, tries to obliterate, control or ultimately restrict any media phenomena and, with the publication of state media and the creation of controlled media with the veneer of independent journalism, inhibits access to information.

SV

NEW FROM SAQI BOOKS

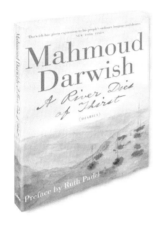

'Darwish speaks of the fight to keep love and vision alive in a world overshadowed by the military-industrial complex, and, as such, is deeply relevant to us all.' *Daily Mail*

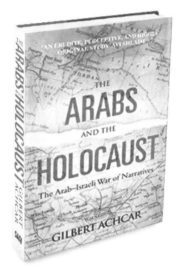

'A work of breath-taking empathy... [A] magisterial study' **Rashid Khalidi**

'Essential reading for anyone who seeks a balanced understanding of the place of Jews and the Holocaust in Arab thinking today.' **Michael R. Marrus**

'A jewel of a memoir' **Maureen Freely**

'Moving and remarkable' **Andrew Finkel**

COPYRIGHT REVOLT

The internet has subverted the laws of intellectual property. **David Allen Green** charts a course through one of the most contentious online issues

Developments in technology and popular culture mean that copyright is now shaping – and in some ways limiting – the scope of freedom of expression. The onerous legal sanctions currently being proposed to protect copyright raise troubling free speech issues. The stand-off between digital rights campaigners and the state looks set to continue, until the law catches up with technology.

The nature of copyright law

From a legal perspective copyright is classed as a property right. This means that the copyrighted work can effectively be bought and sold; and it also means it can be licensed. This allows the copyright owner to define and impose what others can do with the work: such controls can range from software end-user licences to so-called digital rights management in DVDs.

The licensee can be in breach of their licence if they use the work in any way not permitted by the owner, and the non-licensee is infringing the copyright if he or she does any unauthorised act of any kind. In both situations, the law treats the user as an infringer, owing compensation to the wronged copyright owner, who can seek to prohibit any unauthorised use.

Consumer rights vs performing rights. Outside the US Supreme Court in Washington, DC, 29 March 2005
Credit: Yuri Gripas/Reuters

In media products, such as films or books, copyright provides most of the bundle of 'rights' which can be transferred or licensed. Without copyright there would not be a basis for much of the entertainment or media industries. It may only be an 'intellectual' property right, with no tangible existence (unlike real property), but it is not difficult to appreciate the intense attachment that certain business interests have to protecting their copyrights: it is all they really have.

Against this commercial anxiety is the sheer technological ease by which data and files can be copied and stored, adapted and developed. There is now a general sense of entitlement to downloading, sharing and re-engineering the works of others. It is almost in the nature of a mass trespass on the private estates of outraged landowners: an outrage all the more painfully felt, for the owners believe the land is only worth trespassing on because of costly investments privately made.

Moreover, copyright not only subsists in 'content' such as books and music, but also in the means by which data itself is transmitted and stored. In the European Union, copyright is the legal protection that protects computer programs themselves. (In the US, this protection can also be provided by patents.) In this way, using unauthorised software to share content can be a copyright infringement, regardless of who owns the actual content.

It is in this contested and rapidly changing cultural and technological environment that the law of copyright is seeking to balance the respective senses of entitlements of both the end user and producer. This provides the context for the consideration of copyright as a free speech issue.

The application of copyright law

The key to the operation of copyright law is that it deals with the extent to which one can make use of works owned by another. If an expression is entirely original, then there should not be any copyright issue. For example, if one independently came up with a story about a young wizard called Harry Potter, then there is nothing as a matter of copyright law which the copyright owner should be able to do to stop you publishing it, though there could be other legal restrictions from trade marks and so on.

Accordingly, this means that copyright is not especially important in respect of the 'classic' examples of those facing legal limits on their free expression: the street protestors and *samizdat* publishers under illiberal regimes.

In such adverse circumstances, the form of protest or the *samizdat* will probably not need to be derived from works owned by someone else: copyright will be the least of the dissident's legal worries. It is also probably safe to presume that a determined dissident can probably give some original form to an urgent demand or grievance. In turn, the oppressor will undoubtedly also have recourse to sanctions far stronger than a mere action for copyright infringement in policing any unwelcome free speech.

The need for protection for free expression, however, cannot be limited to such entirely original statements. For every protester and publisher there is a need for the content to be reported and transmitted, and it is here that free speech and copyright can clash.

For example, news reporting will often require that incriminated documents are quoted – or even disclosed entirely – rather than summarised. Indeed, without such substantiation there may not be any useful story to publish or broadcast. But the person or entity about to be exposed could, just by asserting copyright, seek to prevent the newspaper or programme from showing its source.

National copyright law usually has a fair use exception for news reporting, and also for criticism and comment. Sometimes such an exception is enough to ensure that a report stands up. But the exception may not extend to the publication, without comment, of entire leaked documents: a publication that is very simple online. Here the law of copyright, as well as the law of confidentiality, can bite and prevent the public disclosure of documents containing information of public interest.

A further issue of copyright use can occur when one uses a work owned by a third party to make a point or just to frame a satire. For example, at the time of writing, there is a fashion on YouTube to use the bunker scene from the war film *Downfall* to portray any once-dominant person in denial during a crisis. This has been done in respect of targets ranging from Hillary Clinton faced with setbacks in the electoral primaries to the chiropractic profession fearful of the prospect of scientific review: it is used for both serious and trivial issues. In principle, however, such so-called mash-ups are at the forbearance of the copyright owner of the framing material.

Similarly, there is a tendency by those who write blogs or contribute to message boards to 'copy and paste' text and other media – often whole articles or files – so as to demonstrate or counter some point. Although the etiquette is to attribute and link to a source, this courtesy would not by itself provide a defence if the use went beyond what would be legally fair to republish. So again, as with mash-ups, such routine activity is actually subject to the whim of the copyright owner of the copied material.

Indeed, the use of derivation and copying is a commonplace in internet-based discussions of public as well as trivial matters. Copyrighted material often provides the cultural forms in which important points can be made and understood. A strict application of copyright law would thereby tend to undermine and limit the scope of public debate.

Such non-commercial use does not really warrant the pejorative labels 'piracy' or 'copyright theft': there is no attempt to commercially resell the original works in a way which deprives the copyright owner of legitimate income. There is no dishonesty, which is the implication of such heated terminology. Instead, the unauthorised use is merely an infringement which causes no commercial damage. Perhaps a licence fee is appropriate; if so, the copyright owner should make it easier for an end user to purchase a licence.

Copyright not only protects the content of an electronic communication; it can also protect the means by which it is transmitted. Unlike more traditional media such as books and newspapers, the software used to transmit and store digital information is itself a work protected by copyright.

Programs, from the operating system on a computer to the Adobe reader used to read documents, are subject to the terms of a software licence. It may be that it is an open-source and enlightened GNU licence, but the principle remains: the use of communication tools themselves raise permission issues not encountered in many other media. The person owning the code can, in effect, prescribe what messages can and cannot be sent.

Copyright and free speech: the way forward

So, in this fluid cultural and technological environment, what should be the position of those who wish to protect free expression and guard against incursions in the name of copyright law?

The first step is to realise that expression does not need to be entirely original to be worthy of free speech protection. As it becomes customary to adopt and develop memes or content owned by others in making serious statements, the free speech activist must seek to ensure that this is not needlessly restricted by the ulterior use of refusing copyright permissions, especially when there is no commercial loss involved.

But more importantly, the free speech activist must be vigilant against the excesses of the reactions of the state and copyright owners, even when unauthorised copying does not actually raise any immediate free expression issues.

The state and copyright owners are increasingly looking to use legal sanctions that are disproportionate and oppressive in policing alleged infringements of copyright. This mismatch between the underlying wrong and the legal consequence naturally concerns those dealing with the limits that the law places on any sharing of information and expression.

In particular, there appears to be a movement by the private interests of copyright owners to extend the criminal sanctions in copyright law from dealing only with unlawful distribution to criminalising infringements by end users. There are even attempts to obtain the legal power to disconnect the internet connections of alleged infringers, regardless of whether it serves an entire household and regardless of the legitimate purposes served by the internet connection. Disconnection is envisaged without the tiresome need to obtain a civil judgment in respect of the infringements.

Whilst it is not for the free speech activist to endorse or facilitate dishonest behaviour, any move to remove the means of communication or penalise expression by coercive legal powers is necessarily a free speech issue.

The granting or exercise of such powers must be opposed when they are disproportionate and illiberal. The criminal and civil law should not seek to prevent access to the internet just because of alleged violations of intellectual property rights, especially where there is no alleged dishonesty or proof of commercial loss. A speech act should not be criminalised just to protect the commercial interests of another.

And such vigilance should not be only in respect of proposed new powers but also to the operation of the law as it stands. In this, copyright joins defamation, confidentiality, privacy, contempt of court, and many other legal actions, as the means by which the illiberal and the culpable can wrongfully curb unwelcome publicity and helpful expression. ❐

©David Allen Green
39(1): 143/148
DOI: 10.1177/0306422010362191
www.indexoncensorship.org

David Allen Green is a freelance writer on legal issues based in London

SAGE Journals Online

Photography© Edmund Sumner 2006

New and Enhanced Features Include

- Improved navigation across the entire platform
- Easy-to-locate, site-level quick search function
- Enhanced advanced search options, including "Fielded Boolean Search"
- Institutional branding on the interface
- RefWorks compatibility

- Improved marked citations, including email, print or save option
- New "My Tools" tab, providing all personalization and alert features in one easy-to-find location
- New and improved contextual "help" system
- Refined search possibilities, including search history and saved searches

http://online.sagepub.com

Safaricom retail stall in Nairobi's Kibera slum, 21 May 2009
Credit: Natasha Elkington/Kenya Business Society/Reuters

RINGING IN CHANGE

News can now be distributed widely in Kenya, but so can hate speech. **Jillo Kadida** reports

The violence that rocked Kenya following the disputed presidential elections at the end of 2007 will always remain in the minds of Kenyans – it claimed more than a thousand lives, uprooted hundreds of thousands of families from their homes and turned neighbours against each other. This was the worst violence the country had ever seen. The events powerfully highlighted the pros and cons of mobile phone technology in Kenya, bringing with it huge advantages and equally huge challenges. During this time, people received up-to-date news and were able to alert others to the conflict's trouble spots, primarily through the use of mobile phones. But phones were also used to spread hate messages, exacerbating an already grave situation. During the post-election violence, several groups used mobile phones to play a vigilante role. Opposition supporters reported on policemen working as poll agents for the ruling Party of National Unity, President Kibaki's party.

This misuse of communication technology has given the government a justification for censoring messages and for introducing legislation to prevent a repeat of the post-election violence. The legislation limits freedom of speech, a primary human right guaranteed under the constitution and international law, citing as its justification the need to maintain public order. This hate speech law places restrictions and limitations on people's opinions and speech. Because the law is unclear about where to draw the line between what is fair comment and what is a hateful message or insult, there is a significant likelihood that the law will be misused and manipulated by politicians during elections to prohibit free expression of public opinion.

Recently, a number of people have been prosecuted on charges of misusing a mobile phone and using it to send hate messages or insults. In October 2009, Regina Nyambura Muniu was handed down a court order after she admitted to sending abusive messages to another woman, Mary Stella Gathoni. The court sentenced her to six months' community service in Nairobi.

The fact that people can be prosecuted for misusing their mobile phones inhibits the population from expressing their opinions without fear. It is unclear whether sending a public officer a text message complaining about shoddy service or telling the officer that he or she is corrupt would amount to misuse or even qualify as hate speech.

Further attempts to restrict mobile phone use have been successfully fought off. During the post-election violence, the government unsuccessfully pushed the largest mobile network, Safaricom, to shut down its SMS service. Today there is a campaign to register all mobile users on security grounds. There's no telling who will have access to this data and how it may be used.

Mobile phones continue to play a vital role in getting news out to the wider public. Many news alert services run on SMS platforms, notifying subscribers of breaking news stories. It has led to further segmentation of news and information content, so that some consumers can choose to receive only political news or business news, sports scores or financial markets data. Most television stations run short text message polls, making their news bulletins interactive. The low cost of sending and receiving SMS messages means this method of receiving information is easily accessible to nearly all sections of society.

For the future, this accessibility may help break down class walls in society. But the tricky part is how to remain vigilant against abuse without using it as an excuse to curtail free expression. ❐

©Jillo Kadida
39(1): 150/152
DOI: 10.1177/03064220103362319
www.indexoncensorship.org

Jillo Kadida is news correspondent for the *Daily Nation*

AGAINST TYRANNY

Michael Scammell on the birth of
Index on Censorship

Lisa Goldman on a drama of censorship

An extract from Gurpreet Kaur Bhatti's
new satire

FREEDOM IS NOT A LUXURY

Michael Scammell, founding editor of *Index on Censorship*, recalls the role of Stephen Spender in the birth of the magazine

My title comes from a brief article that Stephen Spender wrote for the very first issue of *Index on Censorship* in the spring of 1972. In describing his motives for engaging in this enterprise, Stephen commented that what the world's intellectual community most needed at a time when governments were suppressing freedom of expression more than ever was 'organs of consciousness' to alert other members of the community to what was going on, much as early Christians had been 'vigilant for other Christians in times of religious persecution'. Changing the metaphor, Stephen went on to speak of the individual's enduring responsibility for others. 'If a writer whose works are banned wishes to be published, and I am in a position to help him … then to refuse to give help is for me to support the censorship. If I complacently accept the idea that freedom is something that happens in some places and is prevented in others, I am implying that freedom is a matter of accident or privilege.' Assent to censorship was to 'support the views of those who hold freedom to be a luxury enjoyed by bourgeois individualists' (this was a dig at Marxist jargon), but worse than that, it was to allow one's own freedom to be abridged by acquiescing in the loss of it by others. *Index*'s appeal to readers would be to take notice of those who were 'censored, banned or imprisoned' and invite those readers to treat these afflictions as their own.

It was characteristic of Stephen to take a fraternal, communitarian approach to persecution. What made him particularly sensitive to the issue was that he was writing against the backdrop of the turbulent events of 1968, a year that is largely remembered in western Europe and America for student sit-ins, street demonstrations, the rise of a new radicalism, and violent reactions against the Vietnam war, but was also the year when the aspirations of the Czechs and Slovaks to secure a modicum of freedom for themselves during the Prague Spring were violently crushed by a Soviet Russian invasion, and when controls were harshly tightened on writers and intellectuals in the Soviet Union itself. Wherever one looked at that time the forces of oppression seemed to be on the march. A military dictatorship had come to power in Greece the preceding year, matching those already in existence in Spain and Portugal, and it was soon to be followed by a similar one in neighbouring Turkey. Communist governments still held sway in all of eastern Europe and much of Asia, and authoritarian regimes reigned in many countries in Africa (including South Africa), and much of South and Central America. Freedom was in retreat, and concepts like the sanctity of civil and human rights were in their infancy. They had arisen, in fact, in response to the spread of tyranny.

Not that such concepts hadn't existed in other forms before. Indeed, the underlying values driving them were not at all new to Stephen, nor was his concern for them unusual. Much of his life had been devoted to progressive causes of one kind or another, and his enduring interest in politics and social ethics had made him ultra-sensitive to repression both in other countries and at home in Britain. As we know from his memoir, *World Within World,* and from John Sutherland's recent biography, he had been torn from an early age between his attraction to Bloomsbury-like introspection and a more active engagement with social and political forces, epitomised by his sympathy for the modernist movement and by his friendship with similarly engaged writers like Christopher Isherwood and W H Auden (though both moved away in later years from their early interest in politics).

In fact, in the 1930s, when Stephen was young, it was impossible for someone of his temperament to ignore the two rising ideologies of fascism and communism, and like most (but far from all) English writers of his generation, he sided with communism. He was heavily influenced in this matter by his stay in Berlin during the early years of the Hitler regime, and then by the outbreak of the Spanish Civil War, a crucial milestone in the

radicalisation of progressive writers from Europe and North and South America, writers as various as André Malraux, Ignazio Silone, Arthur Koestler, Ernest Hemingway, John Dos Passos, Pablo Neruda, Octavio Paz, and the English writers, E M Forster, John Lehmann, W H Auden, C Day Lewis, Cyril Connolly, George Orwell, Christopher Caudwell, and others.

Battling for the mind of Europe

The 1930s were notable for a parallel development that also influenced Stephen and gave rise to some of the ideas that led ultimately to the establishment of *Index on Censorship,* namely the rise of international solidarity among writers of a certain disposition and the role played by the International PEN Club. This organisation had been founded as early as 1921 in reaction to the terrible hostilities unleashed in Europe by the First World War and the Russian revolution, and the resulting schisms in the way culture and history were being interpreted. It was a novel concept, and in its early years PEN operated very much as a 'club', but after 1933, under the leadership of H G Wells, PEN was radicalised. That year, after a fiery speech by Wells, the pro-Nazi German centre was voted out at PEN's international congress in Dubrovnik, and Wells invoked the concept of 'intellectual freedom', both as a guiding principle of PEN and a stick with which to beat the repressive regimes of Hitler's Germany and Franco's Spain. PEN was undoubtedly left-leaning and communists generally got the benefit of the doubt, partly on the basis of their progressive rhetoric. Both Wells and PEN's vice-president, George Bernard Shaw, made well publicised visits to the Soviet Union, and having been carefully shielded from the reality of Soviet life, returned full of praise for the new kind of society that they had just been shown.

In truth, the Soviet leaders and their intellectual servants were already masters of deception. Campaigns for this or that progressive individual or group were conducted (and manipulated) in western Europe and America in the 1930s, as the communists concealed the true nature of Soviet life behind a curtain that was growing more and more impermeable with each succeeding year, while justifying their policies on the basis of anti-fascism. When the cataclysm of the Second World War put an end to fascism (except for some remnants in southern Europe and Latin America), the situation changed. True, communism itself gained immensely in strength and influence as a result of the war, but despite the initial reluctance (and in some cases refusal) of the European and American left to face up to it, the repressive nature of Soviet society became increasingly visible, and the resulting ideological struggle between liberal democracy and revolutionary communism took the form of the cold war. The cold war split intellectuals in the West in a new way and presented a real dilemma for leftists who, like the French during the Popular Front in the 1930s, felt there should be *pas d'ennemis à la gauche* (no enemies on the left). Nevertheless, a majority, including Stephen Spender, sided with America and western Europe, while a significant minority, especially in France and Italy, sided with the communists. International PEN, like other organisations, reflected that split. Since national PEN centres were now located not only in the liberal democracies, or would-be liberal democracies, but also in the Soviet satellite countries of eastern and central Europe: East Germany, Poland, Czechoslovakia, Hungary, Romania, Bulgaria, and so on (though surprisingly, there was never one in the Soviet Union itself), there was a potential for real conflict, especially when these centres found sympathisers among third world centres influenced by anti-colonial and therefore anti-western sentiment.

The ensuing competition between the two main political blocs during the years of the cold war was often carried out in the form of international cultural conferences, several of them organised soon after the war by the Soviet-controlled Cominform. One of the most celebrated of these, held in France, featured such famous and popular luminaries as Charlie Chaplin, Paul Robeson, Picasso, and Romain Rolland among their star participants. The Americans riposted by organising conferences of their own, the most important of which was the 'Congress for Cultural Freedom', held in 1950 in Soviet-blockaded West Berlin (then surviving thanks to an American airlift). This conference, intended to demonstrate the vitality of western culture, was not as well peopled with celebrities as the French one, but had plenty of intellectual muscle. Tennessee Williams, Carson McCullers, Sidney Hook and Arthur Schlesinger Jr came from America; Claude Mauriac and Jules Romain from France; Ignazio Silone and Carlo Levi from Italy; and A J Ayer, Herbert Read and Hugh Trevor-Roper from England, plus Arthur Koestler (the star of the show), who was sort of stateless, but then living in France.

Stephen didn't go to the Berlin conference, but he was obviously thinking along the same lines. Two years beforehand he had written an article for the *New York Times* entitled 'We *Can* Win the Battle for the Mind of Europe', and a year before the congress he had attended a PEN conference in Venice to express similar ideas. He had also contributed an essay to the anthology *The God that Failed,* edited by Richard Crossman and Arthur Koestler, that was a bestseller in England and America. In common with Koestler, Silone and the other contributors, Stephen described the reasons for his earlier involvement with communism and also his reasons for abandoning it, including a resistance to the conformity of thought imposed on members by the party and the party's hostility to a free literature. He cited a Russian professor who once said to him: 'We cannot afford to have good writers' because 'our best poets write poems which depress the people by expressing a suicidal sense of the purposelessness of life. But we want people to work as they have never done before, so we cannot permit writers to say that they are unhappy.' Stephen couldn't possibly agree with such a credo, and deeply believed that the policy of centring art on politics 'would, in the long run, mean the complete destruction of art'.

The Congress for Cultural Freedom soon turned itself into a permanent organisation of the same name and, a few years later, launched literary and political magazines in Britain, France, Germany and Italy. The British magazine, started in 1953, was called *Encounter,* and Stephen was an obvious choice as an English literary editor to partner the American political editor, Irving Kristol, in running it. Kristol was later replaced by Mel Lasky, founder and former editor of a similar German magazine, *Der Monat,* and for ten years or more *Encounter* was one of the best (if not *the* best) literary and political magazines in the English-speaking world. In 1966, however, its reputation was seriously tarnished (along with the reputation of its editors) when it was revealed that it had been funded from its very beginning by the CIA, and Stephen resigned with a sense of having been exploited and betrayed.

I won't rehearse that long drawn out scandal here, for it has been much written about already. Suffice it to say that like other left-leaning intellectuals at the time, among whom I count myself, I too was shocked and outraged by the disclosures, though in the course of working on my biography of Arthur Koestler, I came to realise that the CIA that funded the Congress for Cultural Freedom in 1950 and *Encounter* starting in 1953 was still in its infancy, and as the successor organisation to America's wartime Office of Strategic Services, staffed by anti-Nazi hands, its leaders were anything but the right-wing ideologues of popular legend. Many of them were quite liberal, in fact, and ran a far different operation from what the CIA had become by 1966, when the outcry started. I would also venture that running a stable of magazines of such high quality as *Encounter* in London, *Preuves* in Paris, and *Der Monat* in Berlin, even if they had a hidden propaganda purpose, was a lot better than most of the things intelligence services did and still do. John Sutherland quotes David Astor, the liberal editor of the *Observer,* as saying that publishing *Encounter* was exactly what the CIA *should* have done, and of course *Encounter*'s harshest critics have had propaganda aims of their own. Still, the deception was serious and carried a heavy price, not least for Stephen, and he had little choice but to resign when he did.

One might have expected him at this point to turn his back entirely on literary activism and cultural diplomacy, but it seems to have become too deeply ingrained for him to abandon it easily. Instead he tried to start a new magazine, a sort of 'son-of-*Encounter*', as John Sutherland puts it, with the support of Isaiah Berlin, Stuart Hampshire, W H Auden, and other stalwarts of the *Encounter* camp. An impressive array of backers and a large amount of support was mustered. The figure of £50,000 per annum was mentioned as a suitable income to aim for, and there was a moment when it seemed within reach, but in the end the effort failed and Stephen turned his attention once more to purely literary matters.

Year of the young rebels

History, however, if I may put it this way, wouldn't leave him alone. One of the more celebrated sit-ins perpetrated by rebellious students in 1968 was the one that occupied the administrative offices of Columbia University. Stephen happened to be in New York at the time, and having been asked by a friend to find the latter's daughter at Columbia to see if she was safe, he ended up climbing through a window to find her. He was so impressed by the youthful idealism and radical arguments of the students he found inside that he published an article about his experience and ended up writing a whole book on the subject, *The Year of the Young Rebels*. His reportorial duties took him from New York to Paris and Prague, and, according to John Sutherland, his book was praised both for its understanding of the roots of this new idealism and for a 'healthy coolness' towards some of the arbitrary violence of its overheated protagonists.

That coolness sprang from a conviction that ultimately the students were not totally serious about their revolt, and their left-wing rhetoric not entirely convincing, but it may also have had something to do with an event that had happened at the very beginning of 1968, and whose implications took a while to sink in. In January that year, *The Times* had published an 'Appeal to World Public Opinion' from two Soviet citizens, Pavel Litvinov and Larisa Bogoraz, asking intellectuals everywhere to condemn the rigged trial of two dissidents and help forestall the expected heavy sentences. The word 'dissident' was still new then and only just coming into vogue, and in fact this was Litvinov and Bogoraz's first 'dissident' act of their own. Unfortunately it didn't help. Their two friends, Alexander Ginzburg and Yuri Galanskov, were sentenced to seven years in the labour camps for doing

Arthur Koestler, Sir Victor Pritchett and Rosamond Lehmann at the 41ˢᵗ International PEN Congress,
24 August 1976. Rosamond Lehmann holds a copy of the first issue of Index on Censorship
Credit: Popperfoto/Getty Images

just the kind of thing that Stephen believed in – publishing a magazine –
and Litvinov and Bogoraz went on to demonstrate publicly in August 1968
against the crushing of the Prague Spring (and earn sentences of their own).

Stephen had no idea, of course, of this later turn of events, when he and
Natasha felt moved to organise a telegram of support in answer to Bogoraz
and Litvinov's appeal. Having obtained the signatures of Auden, A J Ayer,
Day-Lewis, Stuart Hampshire, Julian Huxley, Mary McCarthy, Henry Moore,
J B Priestley and Bertrand Russell, among others, they expressed a readiness
to help 'by any means open to us' and sent it to Litvinov. The text of the
telegram was also broadcast by the BBC Russian Service, and as I have said,
didn't help the unfortunate Ginzburg and Galanskov, especially the latter,
who died in the labor camps. The publicity did seem to help Litvinov and

Bogoraz, however, who were sent into Siberian exile rather than imprisoned and, eight months later, Litvinov unexpectedly responded.

Citing the telegram's offer of help, Litvinov wrote that he and his fellow human rights activists would like to think of it not as a 'rhetorical phrase' but as a genuine offer of assistance. He went on to ask for the creation of an 'international committee' of 'progressive writers, scholars, artists and public personalities' to support the 'democratic movement in the USSR,' and added: 'Of course this committee should not have an anti-communist or anti-Soviet character. It would even be good if it contained people persecuted in their own countries for pro-communist or independent views.' The important point was to oppose violence in the pursuit or defense of any particular ideology, and not solely communist ideology.

Litvinov's letter was a sort of challenge to Stephen and his co-signatories: put your money where your mouth is, and Stephen was energised enough to disregard his earlier *Encounter* disappointment and throw himself again into a new cause. Together with Stuart Hampshire he approached David Astor, the crusading editor of the *Observer,* for financial support, and Astor, who had distanced himself from Stephen's 'son-of-*Encounter*' endeavour, this time willingly agreed. Together they rounded up another impressive group of intellectuals for the board, including Louis Blom-Cooper, Edward Crankshaw, Lord Gardiner, Elizabeth Longford and Sir Roland Penrose, with Dame Peggy Ashcroft, Sir Peter Medawar, Henry Moore, Iris Murdoch, Sir Michael Tippett and Angus Wilson as patrons. They formed an organisation called Writers and Scholars International (WSI), which not only echoed the name of the still new Amnesty International but was envisaged as a sort of sister body, or even a subdivision of Amnesty. Astor had agreed to contribute £5,000 per annum from his personal trust, and they advertised for a director.

It was at this point that I entered the scene. I wasn't the first name on the list. I wasn't even sure I wanted the job. I was holed up in a Kent cottage making my first stab at a biography of Alexander Solzhenitsyn. I had earlier translated books by Tolstoy, Dostoevsky and Nabokov from Russian into English, and had recently translated my first work (*My Testimony* by Anatoly Marchenko) by a Soviet dissident, of which there were to be many afterwards. After a visit from Edward Crankshaw and a formal interview with the board, together with the offer of an exceedingly modest salary, I agreed to give it a try, and I still remember vividly my ride back to Waterloo Station with Martin Ennals, then director of Amnesty International, who had been on the interview committee. He had one of those streamlined black Citroen sedans with pillowy suspension that rose and fell with each bump in the

spring 1972　　　　　　**50p**

road and lurched round corners, and we discussed a proposal by the board to make WSI a subsidiary of Amnesty. Among other things it would help WSI's precarious financial situation, but I quickly grasped between lurches that Martin was uncomfortable at the thought of having such a cuckoo in the nest, and I was equally unhappy at the idea of being the cuckoo. Well before we reached our destination, the idea was jettisoned by joint consent.

Since I have described these events and their consequences in detail elsewhere ('How Index on Censorship Started', in George Theiner, ed., *They Shoot Writers, Don't They?* Faber and Faber), I won't continue this narrative at length. As I wrote in my earlier article, 'there was no programme, other than Litvinov's letter, there were no premises or staff, and there was very little money'. In due course I found a small, windowless office behind a potato merchant's showroom in Covent Garden (this was when it was still a market and well before its transformation into a tourist mecca). I was part time, but even so the cost of an equally part-time assistant (Jenefer Coates), the rent and our modest furnishings ate up quite a bit of our £5,000, and I had to devise a programme that was feasible on a shoestring. Litvinov had proposed two possible forms of action. One was to launch protests and appeals defending individuals against persecution for their beliefs and writings, the other was to inform world public opinion about them and publish some of their censored texts. Given our limited funds, I decided to let Amnesty take care of the protests and appeals and to see if we could manage the second option.

The birth of *Index on Censorship*
In taking this course I had a goal of my own, namely to fulfill a secret desire to edit a literary publication of my own (the only thing I had edited before that was the student newspaper at Nottingham University – though it did win a national prize), and since I had read about Stephen's travails with the CIA and his attempt to start a new journal, I thought he might look kindly on a similar, if much less ambitious, venture along similar lines. Moreover, though I hadn't known Stephen at the time of the *Encounter* affair, I fully sympathised with his sense of betrayal (for *Encounter* had been a highly liberal journal in most of its editorial policies, despite its sources of income), and I had hopes of starting what I thought of as a 'counter-*Encounter*', one with a narrower and purer mandate, namely to oppose and combat censorship by all peaceful means possible, without the encumbrance of any sort of government backing.

Actually, the CCF itself had earlier had the same idea and for a brief period published a sister magazine to *Encounter* called simply *Censorship,* but the public had been barely aware of it (I certainly wasn't until I started my new job with WSI), and it folded after the CIA scandal. Unaware of this at the time, I proposed to the WSI board that we start a modest newspaper or journal of our own, and after a brief discussion I was given the go-ahead. I'm bound to say that this circumstance undercuts the idea that Stephen was the begetter of *Index*, for the original idea was mine, as was the name, but of course it was Stephen who had set in motion the entire process leading to its establishment, and his enthusiastic endorsement and support were crucial to whatever success it enjoyed.

I have written in that earlier article about how we arrived at our title and format, and how we put our first few issues together, all with Stephen's participation, but the important point is that he and I saw absolutely eye to eye on the nature of our mission. We still felt that the US and its allies, including Britain, were fundamentally correct in their opposition to Soviet expansionism and Soviet ideology, and we endorsed the principle of a cold (as opposed to hot) war of ideas to further that aim. At the same time, we regarded other aspects of American and British foreign policy as short-sighted and counterproductive, namely the tendency to go easy on, or even support, authoritarian right-wing regimes such as those run by Franco in Spain, Salazar in Portugal, or the Shah of Iran, simply because these regimes were anti-communist. *Encounter*'s sin had consisted not in supporting those regimes, but rather in remaining silent about them, and we were determined not to undercut our moral authority by sacrificing our core values. In this we felt we were in complete harmony with Litvinov's recommendations, convinced that an impartial hostility to censorship wherever we found it (including, on occasion, England and America) would carry more weight everywhere, even in the Soviet Union, than would a selective, one-sided approach.

I hope to write more one day about the early history of *Index,* but let me conclude by saying that while he was often away from London because of his lecturing and literary work, Stephen was always on call when we needed him, either to connect us with other writers and translators, offer political advice, or help with the tedious business of fundraising. He was our patron saint, the public face of *Index*, and the best tribute I can think of to his contribution is the continuing success of the magazine we founded together. I never dreamed it would last so long and grow so fruitfully, and I'm delighted to see its durability. In a brief preface to the collection of articles I mentioned earlier, *They Shoot Writers, Don't They?* (published, appropriately, in 1984), Stephen reformulated one of the ideas he had put forward in the first issue of the magazine. 'Despite the views of ideologists,' he wrote, 'we are none of us creatures of the political systems in which we live. We are all of us human beings, individuals. What happens to individuals over there, living in their world of totalitarian dictatorships (taking different forms in different countries) tells us something about what is happening to ourselves. For we are all dimly aware that on some level of our consciousness, what happens to people in concentration camps and prisons happens also to us.'

It required a positive act of will to imagine what it was like for writers and others to live under tyranny, to have their words suppressed and be persecuted for even expressing them, and it was one of Stephen's gifts, with the empathy of a true poet, not only to be able to imagine them but also to act on his insights and attempt to alleviate them. His informed concern for suffering fellow writers (and through them for suffering individuals everywhere) is a fitting reminder of his deep and abiding humanity, and the founding of *Index on Censorship* was a small token of that. ❐

©Michael Scammell
This is an edited and expanded version of a talk delivered to the Stephen Spender Centenary Conference in London on 26 February 2009
39(1): 155/167
DOI: 10.1177/0306422010362321
www.indexoncensorship.org

Michael Scammell edited *Index on Censorship* from 1972–80. His biography of Arthur Koestler, *Koestler: the Indispensable Intellectual*, is published by Faber & Faber. He is the author of *Solzhenitsyn, A Biography* and has translated numerous books from Russian, including Nabokov's *The Defense*. He teaches at Columbia University

NEW FROM TELEGRAM

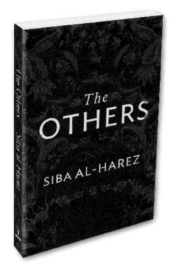

An explosive portrayal of life for a young lesbian in Saudi Arabia.

'Claustrophobic setting and exquisite eroticism simultaneously drain and exhilarate.' *Guardian*

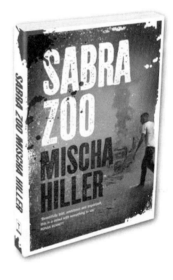

'A defiant, stunning debut' *Guardian*

'A searing and accomplished novel that takes the reader back to the bloody events in Beirut in summer 1982 during the Israeli invasion of Lebanon.' *Saudi Gazette*

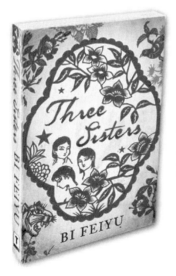

'A thrilling family epic that depicts China's dispossessed longings and love.' Xiaolu Guo

BEHUD: A WRITER REPLIES

Lisa Goldman talks to Index about directing
Gurpreet Kaur Bhatti's satire on censorship

The fate of Gurpreet Kaur Bhatti's play Behzti *became a byword for censorship when its run was cancelled at the Birmingham Repertory Theatre in 2004, following protests by members of the Sikh community, who objected to the dramatisation of rape set in a temple (Gurdwara). Bhatti's new play,* Behud*, is a satire of what can happen when contemporary theatre collides with politics and religion.* An exclusive extract from the play follows the interview.

Lisa Goldman: The play is about a writer called Tarlochan, who is trying to write about a previous play of hers that was closed down. What we see is her attempt to construct the various characters involved and their relationships with one another, but also their relationships with her as the writer. At first she's the invisible hand, driving their intentions and motivations, but sometimes they do things she doesn't want them to do, they become much more wilful than she'd ever intended or expected. The situation becomes reversed, so that the characters come to control her and her play is threatened with closure.

Index: Can you tell me about the genesis of the play?

Lisa Goldman: Originally, Gurpreet [Bhatti] brought me a very rough first draft. It's quite normal in theatre for a writer to bring you something they're particularly passionate about, to see if you like it or not. At this early stage, the piece was very much a linear satire about a fictional event where a playwright's work is censored. It had very much the same characters as the final piece. It's moved from a linear satire, where the writer is just one of ten or 11 characters, to the writer becoming part of the process of constructing the play.

She's giving a platform to all of these characters, but at the same time you're seeing it from the dark, subjective perspective of the writer trapped within the situation. I find that very interesting as an artist. Not just in terms of the political-social situation, but in terms of creating a piece of artistic work. The self-censorship, the control you exert on yourself or not, working on all those levels just seems so much more interesting.

Index: This is very much a play about control, or the illusion of control – whether it's in the theatre or outside the theatre.

Lisa Goldman: That's one of the reasons I wanted to do it, because I was disgusted by what happened, by the theatre industry, which I'm part of. I thought when she brought me that first draft, 'You deserve your right to reply on what's happened, because the theatre industry silenced you, didn't support you.' Why weren't we up there in coach loads? Why did it take everyone by surprise? Why have we become so lazy in our engagement in activism around that issue?

Index: Looking back, what do you think should have happened differently?

Lisa Goldman: I think they should have kept the play running. I think they should have protected the staff. I think if they needed to close down the pantomime in order to keep the play running, then they should have done that. I thought it was appalling personally. It's a very slippery slope to say: 'This is a bit difficult, let's not worry about freedom of speech on this issue because it's a volatile situation.' Where does that take you?

Index: In Gurpreet Bhatti's new play, the character of the author, Tarlochan, tries to make the protesters understand that this is not a real Sikh temple being defiled. She's trying to make it clear to them it's theatre, but at the same time, she's having to learn a very horrible lesson about the impact on reality of something she thinks is contained within fiction.

Lisa Goldman: This is always a very interesting question. It's a very easy get out to say this is a work of fiction, a work of the imagination. But it is more complicated than that, because works of the imagination sometimes contain a deeper truth than works of reality, so they do represent reality. If it did have no bearing on reality, why would it create such friction in the first place? These works go into that side of our minds that we would rather not look at, and theatre does that in a particularly public way.

People can take offence at all sorts of things in theatre, from language used to acts of violence, to the extent where they think they've seen something on stage when in fact they haven't, they've only seen it in their mind. I've witnessed that many times on a number of shows, and it's always really fascinating. I remember producing a play called *Stitching* by Anthony Neilsen and a journalist writing about it afterwards maintained there was a scene where a character was masturbating over pictures of the Holocaust, which was absolutely not in there. That's the picture talked about on stage and in their imagination they really believed they had seen it. It's just a very powerful medium in that way.

Index: If you're writing something contemporary about a minority group that has issues about its own identity in a culture, then there can be a perception within that group that they somehow own the work of art. We saw this with *Behzti* and with Monica Ali's *Brick Lane*.

Lisa Goldman: I think it comes back to this sort of notion of responsibility – what responsibility you have as an artist in terms of representing your own or another community. It's really difficult because it depends on the kind of play you're doing. I always make an effort to authenticate work when I direct it to avoid what the director does in *Behud* and have Arab writing on the tins when it's completely inappropriate. I think that's a very interesting moment. I think the flipside of that is that people should be free to write what they want and not feel a responsibility. I think it's the difference between the authentication culturally and a representation of a particular notion of that culture that is deemed by self-appointed guardians to be most acceptable.

I just did a play called *Shraddha* about the Romany, which included a character whose husband has left her. That's very unusual within the Romany community, and it would be very, very frowned on. Does that mean it couldn't happen or has never happened? No, but if that had been asked of Romanies before that play had been commissioned, some might say: 'You can't put that in, it doesn't happen.'

Drama is always about the experiences that don't normally happen, that are on the edge of common experience. I think I'm stating the obvious really, but as a writer and a director that boundary between being responsible to a cultural reality and at the same time being completely free to invent – that is the kind of line you are treading. That generally doesn't feel problematic, it's clear where that line is. I think the problem which comes with that interface is with members of a community who are unhappy about what you've written, and that's clearly what happened with *Behzti*.

Index: Do you think that the arts face a continuing crisis in terms of religion and censorship?

Lisa Goldman: I think it's really hard to second guess what's going to happen in the future, but all you can say is that unless you keep pushing the boundaries of what is seen to be acceptable, those boundaries will get pushed back. So you have to constantly be vigilant about the kind of programming you're doing. I think we can see from the atmosphere of fundamentalism and the desire to be offended, actually, that it's prevalent at the moment.

Index: The desire to be offended?

Lisa Goldman: Yes, the desire to be offended. That feels to me that that's a part of the atmosphere of the moment.

Index: You've been working on this for two years with Gurpreet Bhatti. What would you say about the journey that the play's made in that time?

Lisa Goldman: I think it's become more deeply personal, raw, and has started to celebrate the subjective, as well as being even handed and viewing events from a distance. And in many ways, that's about being less controlling as a writer in a way: allowing your own vulnerabilities as a writer to be there, not simply looking at a writer-character who's been the victim of a situation, but almost taking a character who is struggling with all her own demons – as all writers do. It's very difficult to write for a public space. Writing a novel is one thing. You write it and then it goes off to your editor and then the next person picks it up. It's a less mediated relationship.

But when it comes to theatre, it is mediated by a director, by the actors and, as we saw with *Behzti*, by a whole institution and a whole other series of layers of political-social machinations. You've got to be very, very strong in all that to keep it together, I think Gurpreet is absolutely extraordinary as a person to have completely kept it together with dignity and total strength and clarity and then to have made the decision to write this play, and go the nth degree with it. She's an incredibly inspiring woman. ❐

Lisa Goldman was talking to Jo Glanville
39(1): 169/173
DOI: 10.1177/0306422010363348
www.indexoncensorship.org

Lisa Goldman is artistic director of Soho Theatre. *Behud* premiers at Belgrade Theatre, Coventry, 27 March–10 April (Box office: 024 7655 3055) and then at Soho Theatre, London, 13 April–8 May (Box office: 020 7478 0100)

BEHUD

An extract from **Gurpreet Kaur Bhatti**'s new play

'Shame on Sikh playwright for her corrupt imagination'
Banner at demonstration against *Behzti*, December 2004

CAST OF CHARACTERS:

TARLOCHAN KAUR GREWAL – playwright

DCI VINCENT HARRIS – a man unhinged

DI GURPAL (GARY) SINGH MANGAT – an all too decent individual

SATINDER SHERGILL – a ravenous reporter

KHUSHWANT SINGH BAINS – an energised adolescent (performed by actor playing GARY)

MR SIDHU – an overly successful businessman

AMRIK – a man to whom life has not been kind

ANDREW FLEMING – artistic director of the Writer's Theatre (performed by actor playing VINCE)

JOANNE STEVENSON – deputy leader of the local council

GIRL (Baby) – a cheeky slip of a thing, aged 10 (performed by actor playing SAT)

MAN – just over from the Punjab, 23 (performed by actor playing AMRIK)

NOTES:
Any resemblance to real events is entirely intentional.
Names have been changed to protect the fictional characters.

Boardroom. ANDREW, JOANNE, SIDHU and AMRIK sit around a huge table. Sounds of the demonstration can be heard outside. In particular there is a loud chant of 'Bole So Nihal'.

AMRIK No actors are getting through that lot. And if they do they might not feel like acting.

JOANNE You assured us it would be a peaceful protest.

SIDHU It is peaceful. They are happy, good boys.

AMRIK We know the play isn't finished.

ANDREW A new piece of theatre is always being developed during rehearsals, that's simply the creative process.

AMRIK Don't patronise us. What's she got planned for the end?

ANDREW I can't inform you of every minute change to the script.

SIDHU The story is so disgusting. It makes me feel like doing ulti.

ANDREW You've already had unprecedented access to Tarlochan's work.

SIDHU You don't care about our feelings Mr Fleming.

ANDREW I do care Mr Sidhu. That's why we're here, trying to sort things out. This play is a piece of fiction. It's not real, do you at least accept that?

AMRIK You have a responsibility to the people whose taxes fund your art.

ANDREW There's nothing in this piece that breaks any law.

AMRIK What's the point of your Writer's Theatre?

ANDREW   It's a place where artists are empowered to explore ideas.

AMRIK   And who decides which artists get to explore these ideas?

ANDREW   Somebody's got to do it.

AMRIK   Somebody who looks like you, somebody who thinks like you
           think …

ANDREW   There's no need to be personal just because you don't agree
           with my choices.

AMRIK   Everything you present about us is your take on who we are.

ANDREW   Look, I don't write the plays.

AMRIK   Do you accept that you don't understand us?

ANDREW   No. Dramatic themes are universal. And good writing is good
           writing wherever it comes from.

SIDHU   I wish someone would write a nice play about a nice subject.

JOANNE   We can't control what people write Mr Sidhu.

*TARL enters. She watches them from the edge of the stage, just outside the
characters' vision.*

SIDHU   Is she keeping it set in the Gurdwara?

ANDREW   Yes.

SIDHU   Please, I'm begging you, ask her to change it to a community
           centre.

TARL   Wait …

The characters start speaking very quickly.

ANDREW   She is aware of your views but she will not compromise the
           setting.

AMRIK	So what are you going to do?
ANDREW	We hope to go ahead as planned.
AMRIK	Are you prepared to delay the opening?
ANDREW	No.
AMRIK	What's the point of this meeting if you're not going to listen?
TARL	Slow down ...
ANDREW	You are being listened to.
JOANNE	I for one am listening.
SIDHU	You have to make some concessions.
ANDREW	We're discussing those issues now.
AMRIK	Tarlochan should be here.
TARL	No, I don't want to ...
JOANNE	He does have a point.
ANDREW	It's not appropriate.
TARL	I'm just painting a picture, I don't have to be in it.
SIDHU	We can't have this meeting without her!

The dialogue reaches a crescendo.

AMRIK	[*shouts*] This is rubbish.

TARL approaches.

AMRIK	All these words, they're rubbish!
TARL	No they're not.

Performances of Behzti *are cancelled at the Birmingham Repertory Theatre, 20 December 2004*
Credit: Darren Staples/Reuters

AMRIK   War! This is war.

TARL   [*shouts*] No it's not.

The characters stand up and look at TARL, she recoils in shock.

ANDREW   Tarlochan, what are you doing here?

TARL   What?

SIDHU   So this is the girl?

JOANNE   At last!

AMRIK   Long time no see.

TARL   This is wrong.

SIDHU   She's much shabbier than I expected.

JOANNE   So you do exist!

TARL   No ... I'm ... I'm not in it.

ANDREW   In what?

TARL   I don't know how to be.

ANDREW   Your being here isn't a good idea.

TARL   I know, but this isn't right, you're not saying the right words.

The characters look at each other, confused.

JOANNE   What's she on about now?

ANDREW   Best if you come back later.

AMRIK   You look like shit. What happened to you?

TARL   I'm not sure what's going on.

SIDHU   Brain damage.

ANDREW   This is a very stressful time for her.

Frozen to the spot, TARL stares at the characters.

TARL   [*urgent*] Stand up, sit down, stand up, sit down ...

Nothing happens.

TARL   Stand up, sit down ...

ANDREW   What are you saying, Tarlochan?

TARL   Stop this now!

ANDREW   I'm sorry but you're going to have to wait outside.

TARL   Outside? Where?

ANDREW   In the corridor.

SIDHU   Please I beg you change it to a community centre.

TARL   What?

SIDHU   Why are you torturing us?

TARL   I don't understand.

AMRIK   She won't talk to you, Uncle.

JOANNE   Can we please get on?

The characters sit back down.

ANDREW   Look it's my duty, my right to support this writer and to produce her work.

SIDHU   Having the right does not mean it is right. The point is that this young lady is a bad apple.

Stunned, TARL observes the characters as the scene continues.

ANDREW   She's an artist, she's going to offend some people. Surely?

SIDHU   So you admit it is offensive! [*a beat*] How long have you lived in this city, Mr Fleming?

ANDREW   Sixteen months.

SIDHU   I have resided here for nearly 50 years. This is my home. And to have such pain inflicted on me in my own home is wrong.

AMRIK   We're the lifeblood of this city, it's us you should be entertaining. Why can't I bring my mum and dad and mates into this building to see a show that means something to us?

ANDREW   You can.

AMRIK   You don't want to include us. This time we're not having it, that's what you can't stand.

ANDREW   I admit we need to do better. That's why I'm trying to include you now.

AMRIK   You don't know how to relate to people like me.

ANDREW   Plenty of my staff come from different ethnic backgrounds.

AMRIK   None of them make decisions though. And most of them are trained to think like you think. The ones who challenge you always end up leaving.

SIDHU   Please, Mr Fleming, realise you are going too far.

ANDREW   Tarlochan is exploring sensitive issues and yes the play might shock some people. That ability to challenge, coupled with decent writing, is what constitutes great theatre. And if you don't understand that simple principle …

SIDHU   You think I'm thick!

JOANNE   Let's all calm down.

TARL   Please … this is going wrong …

JOANNE   Will you stop butting in?

ANDREW   I really think you should wait outside.

TARL   Yes, okay. Maybe I'll go and come back … and then things'll be back to normal.

ANDREW   Whatever makes you feel comfortable.

Perplexed TARL half nods. The characters watch her exit.

AMRIK   We are also here to protect Tarlochan. She's still one of us and we've heard certain things.

ANDREW   What things?

SIDHU   Sadly there are a few hotheads amongst our number who are
          not satisfied by talking.

JOANNE   Then you must deal with them.

AMRIK   Thought you cared about her.

ANDREW   It's not my role to scaremonger.

JOANNE   If there was anything significant the police would know.

Andrew's phone rings. He checks the screen.

ANDREW   I'll be back.

AMRIK   Who's left, Mr Fleming?

ANDREW   What?

AMRIK   To care about her.

ANDREW exits.

JOANNE   Would anyone like some tea?

SIDHU   No tea.

AMRIK   So what now, Joanne?

SIDHU   You think I have fought this hard to make my home here that
          I will stop fighting just because of what that man says.

JOANNE   What do you mean by fighting?

AMRIK   What do you mean by it?

JOANNE doesn't respond.

AMRIK   With the use of modern communications, ordinary people have
          the power to become generals of their own armies. Anyone
          anywhere could receive a call to arms.

JOANNE   That kind of talk might get Andrew all hot and bothered but I'm afraid it doesn't faze me.

SIDHU   All Amrik means is that systems are in place.

AMRIK'S phone rings. He takes the call and goes to the side.

SIDHU   You know, Joanne, I think you are a nice lady.

JOANNE   Thank you.

SIDHU   I have always supported you and I have always urged the residents of your ward to support you. What I have done is like asking people to keep buying the same washing powder, even though there is another cheaper, better washing powder on the shelf. Do you know why I ask them?

JOANNE   Because we share common principles.

SIDHU   No. Because we respect each other. And we have an understanding which we must never acknowledge.

JOANNE   Mr Sidhu …

SIDHU   An unspoken, indefinable understanding. Like it is always in the air. Like it is air. How can you expect people to buy a washing powder which stains their clothes?

JOANNE   Mr Sidhu, I think we should keep artistic matters separate from community matters.

SIDHU   That is the exact problem, they have been kept separate. Artistic issues must be monitored, otherwise people can go round making things up.

AMRIK comes off the phone.

AMRIK   Word on the street is the home secretary wants this whole thing calmed down, he doesn't need his visit overshadowed by some stupid play.

JOANNE   The police will ensure things remain calm.

AMRIK   I reckon the opening will be delayed.

JOANNE   It won't. [*a beat*] I can see how passionately you both feel but I'm afraid I won't budge. The play's going on without any changes, and that's final.

AMRIK   No one's listening to us, Joanne.

JOANNE   I am. Let the play happen and you will be perceived as the dignified, tolerant community the country knows you to be. By getting all fired up you're giving Tarlochan and her work even more publicity.

AMRIK   [*to Sidhu*] She's trying to manipulate you.

JOANNE   Your presence makes her seem more exciting. I don't believe for one minute she's this brilliant writer. If the play is shown, people will see the flaws in the writing and her own work will expose her as the mediocre artist she really is. So in a funny way, you'll be proved right. But to stop her having her say, that just isn't possible.

ANDREW comes back in, he's visibly agitated and approaches AMRIK.

ANDREW   Your demonstrators have been threatening my box office staff.

AMRIK   They're probably overwhelmed by the sight of more than one brown face in the queue.

ANDREW   Those workers just about earn the minimum wage. None of this is their fault.

TARL enters and marches up to the middle of the stage.

SIDHU   Maybe you should pay your staff more.

ANDREW   Your friends out there are baying for blood. I want you out.

TARL   No! Ask them to stay, they're supposed to stay!

Nothing happens. All the characters watch TARL who is becoming increasingly distressed.

ANDREW   Did the police forget your lunch?

TARL   Why aren't you saying what I'm writing?

SIDHU   I told you, she has brain problems.

A fraught TARL goes up to AMRIK and takes the gun out of his pocket.

JOANNE   Shouldn't the police be with her?

TARL assumes a shooting position.

JOANNE   Oh, my God.

The characters leap to their feet and shout and scream in fear. ANDREW'S arms fly up in surrender. MR SIDHU immediately lies on the floor face down. TARL fires the gun into space but only a few sorry clicks sound. In despair, TARL drops the gun. AMRIK quickly retrieves it. The characters breathe a collective sigh of relief. ANDREW angrily turns to TARL.

ANDREW   Have you lost your mind?

TARL   I was just trying something.

ANDREW   [to AMRIK] How dare you bring a firearm into my building.

AMRIK   I didn't even know it was there. She must have planted it on me.

TARL   It's only pretend, you can check.

AMRIK checks it and nods.

JOANNE   That was not funny, young lady!

SIDHU   We could press charges.

ANDREW   She didn't mean anything by it, did you Tarlochan?

TARL   No.

ANDREW   She's under a great deal of pressure.

AMRIK   Things are going to get a lot worse.

ANDREW   Will you please leave?

SIDHU   Mark my words, this story is not finished yet!

AMRIK and SIDHU head out. A shocked ANDREW turns to TARL.

ANDREW   What the hell were you thinking?

TARL   I don't know.

JOANNE   We can hardly accuse them of intimidating behaviour while you're trying to murder us all.

ANDREW   Quite.

TARL   Sorry.

ANDREW   Anyway, we're fucked.

ANDREW sits down and rubs his eyes. He downs a jug of water.

ANDREW   The police have asked me to delay the opening by an hour.

TARL   No!

JOANNE   [*shocked*] What?

ANDREW   They're totally outnumbered, most of their officers are protecting your bloody man.

JOANNE   This is unbelievable.

ANDREW   They can't assure the safety of the actors. I've no choice. You've got to convince these people, Joanne.

JOANNE   They think they can bully me, after everything I've done for them. Well they bloody well can't.

ANDREW'S phone rings. He turns it off.

ANDREW   I'm late for rehearsal. Are you coming, Tarlochan?

TARL   I'll ... er ... be there in a bit.

ANDREW heads out. Aghast, TARL sits down.

JOANNE   Is there any tea going?

ANDREW   I'll find someone to bring it up.

A shaken TARL watches ANDREW exit.

JOANNE   Try not to worry about the demonstration.

TARL   Am I still me?

JOANNE   Must be hard, I mean for your life to be threatened ...

TARL   ... or am I writing me?

JOANNE   Rest assured that you have the council's unequivocal support. I can imagine how you must be feeling. As a woman in politics one is constantly doing battle. One needs tenacity, self-belief, stamina.

TARL   Is my play still happening?

JOANNE   No question. Don't worry about your friendly neighbourhood Sikhs, they'll do as they're told. I mean why shouldn't you attack what's wrong with your culture ...

TARL   There's nothing wrong with my culture. No more than with yours.

JOANNE   I blame the parents. Parents across cultures. Do you know that poem, they fuck you up your mum and dad ...?

TARL   Yes.

JOANNE   I hear you write for 'The Bill'?

TARL   Used to.

JOANNE   Do you get to meet all the stars?

TARL   Is there any food here?

JOANNE   I've no idea.

TARL   The police are supposed to bring me a sandwich and some crisps.

JOANNE   Andrew said you encouraged his discussions with the Sikhs.

TARL   Maybe I hoped there might be some brown faces in the audience.

JOANNE   You got that one wrong, they're all outside the building. Surely telling them about the story and the setting was a mistake?

TARL   I wanted my words to go into their heads.

JOANNE   What about your family? [*pause*] Well these days your friends are your family.

TARL   There's nobody.

JOANNE   So what drove you to write the play?

TARL   I always felt like planting a bomb.

JOANNE   Sounds a bit foolhardy!

TARL   Why do you do what you do?

JOANNE   Well I left my career for politics because I care about people and I want a better society.

TARL   You should have stayed in teaching.

JOANNE   How do you know I was a teacher?

TARL   You look like a drunk with a job.

JOANNE   You're very … contrary.

TARL	Things just sort of come out of me.
JOANNE	There are people outside who want you dead because of what comes out of you. Why focus your writing on your community? Why put yourself in this position?
TARL	I won't pretend they don't exist. I am of them. And they are of me. I'm much more like them than you think.
JOANNE	You've lost me now.
TARL	It's not my job to be sensitive and considerate. I hate the quiet softness and tranquillity that people yearn for.
JOANNE	There's a terrible sense of unease about you. Dis-ease. Like Disease.

ANDREW comes back in.

ANDREW	I can't find anyone to make the tea.
JOANNE	You make it.
ANDREW	I don't know how to work the urn.
JOANNE	You must have been camping as a boy.
TARL	Is the play still happening?
ANDREW	Of course.
JOANNE	Of course.
ANDREW	We're going up late that's all.

Sound of police sirens.

TARL	That might be my lunch. [*a beat*] I'm sorry for the way I am. And I appreciate everything you're doing. I won't say it again.
JOANNE	You have my word, Tarlochan, I'll fight for you and your play with every breath in my body.
TARL	I'll pray that you keep breathing.

JOANNE   You don't really pray?

TARL   Twice a day.

JOANNE   Just when you thought things couldn't get any weirder!

ANDREW   [to TARL] The actors are having difficulties with the onion scene.

TARL stares at him.

ANDREW   The lines keep getting stuck in their throats. Could you go through it with them? They're in the studio.

TARL   Okay.

They watch TARL exit. ANDREW turns to JOANNE.

ANDREW   So, what do you think?

JOANNE   At best funny peculiar, at worst intolerably rude. Probably bipolar.

ANDREW   I'm afraid true talent is rarely pretty.

JOANNE   You can say that again. She'd be a prime candidate for Gok's Fashion Fix. ❐

© Gurpreet Kaur Bhatti
30(1): 174/191
DOI: 10.1177/0306422010363347
www.indexoncensorship.org